THE COMMONWEALTH AND INTERNATIONAL LIBRARY

Joint Chairmen of the Honorary Editorial Advisory Board

SIR ROBERT ROBINSON, O.M., F.R.S., LONDON

DEAN ATHELSTAN SPILHAUS, MINNESOTA

PERGAMON OXFORD ENGLISH SERIES

General Editor: D. MATTAM

WAR POETRY: AN ANTHOLOGY

WAR POETRY:
AN ANTHOLOGY

EDITED WITH INTRODUCTION & COMMENTARIES

D. L. JONES

HEAD OF ENGLISH DEPARTMENT

ST. ALBANS BOYS' GRAMMAR SCHOOL

PERGAMON PRESS

OXFORD · NEW YORK · TORONTO

SYDNEY · BRAUNSCHWEIG

Pergamon Press Ltd., Headington Hill Hall, Oxford

Pergamon Press Inc., Maxwell House, Fairview Park, Elmsford,
New York 10523

Pergamon of Canada Ltd., 207 Queen's Quay West, Toronto 1

Pergamon Press (Aust.) Pty. Ltd., 19a Boundary Street,
Rushcutters Bay, N.S.W. 2011, Australia

Vieweg & Sohn GmbH, Burgplatz 1, Braunschweig

First edition 1968

Reprinted 1970

Library of Congress Catalog Card No. 67–28670

Printed in Great Britain by A. Wheaton & Co., Exeter

08 012622 7 (flexicover)
08 012621 9 (hard cover)

CONTENTS

ACKNOWLEDGEMENTS

The Editor is grateful to the following for permission to use copyright material:

Mr. Barry Amiel for "Death is a Matter of Mathematics" by Barry Amiel, from *Poems from India* (Oxford University Press).

Mr. Peter Appleton for "The Responsibility".

Faber & Faber Ltd. for "The Quarry" from *Collected Shorter Poems* by W. H. Auden. Copyright 1937 and renewed 1964 by W. H. Auden. Reprinted from *The Collected Poetry of W. H. Auden* by permission of Random House, Inc.

The Society of Authors as the literary representative of the Estate of the late Laurence Binyon for "For the Fallen" by Laurence Binyon.

Mr. Charles Causley and Rupert Hart-Davis Ltd. for "Death of an Aircraft" from *Union Street* by Charles Causley.

Miss D. E. Collins and Methuen & Co. Ltd. for "Elegy in a Country Churchyard" from *Collected Poems of G. K. Chesterton*. Reprinted by permission of Dodd, Mead & Company, Inc. from *The Collected Poems of G. K. Chesterton*. Copyright 1932 by Dodd, Mead & Company, Inc.

The Trustees of the Hardy Estate, The Macmillan Company of Canada Ltd. and Macmillan & Co. Ltd. for "In Time of 'The Breaking of Nations' " and "Christmas, 1924" from *The Collected Poems of Thomas Hardy*, and for the extract from *The Dynasts*. "Christmas, 1924" reprinted with permission of The Macmillan Company of New York from *Winter Words* by Thomas Hardy. Copyright 1928 by Florence E. Hardy and Sydney C. Cockerell. Renewed 1956 by Lloyds Bank Ltd. The Extract from *The Dynasts* reprinted by courtesy of St. Martin's Press, Inc.

Faber & Faber Ltd. for "Six Young Men" from *The Hawk in the Rain* by Ted Hughes. Reprinted by permission of Harper & Row, Publishers.

Faber & Faber Ltd. for "Eighth Air Force" from *Selected Poems* by Randall Jarrell. Reprinted by permission of Mrs. Randall Jarrell.

The Hogarth Press and Jonathan Cape Ltd. for "The Nabara" from *Collected Poems 1954* by C. Day Lewis. Copyright 1933, 1961 by C. Day Lewis. Reprinted by permission of the Harold Matson Company, Inc.

Faber & Faber Ltd. for "Convoy" from *Collected Poems* by Louis MacNeice. Reprinted by permission of Oxford University Press, Inc.

Mr. Harold Owen and Chatto & Windus Ltd. for "The Parable of the Old Men and the Young", "Spring Offensive", "Anthem for Doomed Youth", "Insensibility" and "The End" from *The Collected Poems of Wilfred Owen*. Copyright © Chatto & Windus Ltd. 1963. Reprinted by permission of New Directions Publishing Corporation.

Mr. Peter Porter and The Scorpion Press Ltd. for "Your Attention Please" by Peter Porter.

Jonathan Cape Ltd. for "Lessons of the War" from *A Map of Verona* by Henry Reed. Copyright 1947, by Henry Reed. Reprinted by permission of Harcourt, Brace and World, Inc.

Mr. Siegfried Sassoon for "The Redeemer", "Suicide in the Trenches" and "Memorial Tablet" from *Collected Poems* by Siegfried Sassoon.

Faber & Faber Ltd. for "Ultima Ratio Regum" from *Collected Poems* by Stephen Spender. Copyright 1942, by Stephen Spender. Reprinted from *Collected Poems 1928–1953*, by Stephen Spender, by permission of Random House, Inc.

Mrs. Helen Thomas and Faber & Faber Ltd. for "This is No Case of Petty Right or Wrong" and "A Private" from *Collected Poems* by Edward Thomas.

Mr. Ruthven Todd and J. M. Dent & Sons Ltd. for "These Are Facts" by Ruthven Todd.

Mr. Rex Warner for "Arms in Spain" by Rex Warner.

Mr. M. B. Yeats and Macmillan & Co. Ltd. for "On Being Asked for a War Poem" and "An Irish Airman Foresees His Death" from *Collected Poems of W. B. Yeats*. Reprinted with permission of the Macmillan Company of New York from *Collected Poems* by W. B. Yeats. Copyright 1919 by the Macmillan Company. Renewed 1946 by Bertha Georgie Yeats.

I should also like to express my personal gratitude to Mrs. P. D'Arcy of the General Studies Association who suggested my undertaking the original course upon which this book is based, and to the other members of the English sub-committee for their help and advice; to Mr. Barry Amiel and Mr. Peter Porter for answering my questions about their poems; to Professor Matthew Hodgart for advice on the texts of the border ballads; to my colleague, Mr. C. C. Warden, for assistance with a number of classical allusions.

I am particularly indebted to Mr. D. Alun Hopkins, who not only read through the book in typescript but offered many helpful suggestions and considerable encouragement; and to my wife, who also read the typescript, corrected mistakes, and has shown patience and understanding throughout the preparation of the book.

D. L. J.

My promise was, and I record it so,
To write in verse (God wot though little worth)
That war seems sweet to such as little know
What comes thereby, what fruits it bringeth forth:
Who knows none evil his mind no bad abhors,
But such as once have felt the scorching fire,
Will seldom efte to play with flame desire.

GEORGE GASCOIGNE (?1525–77)

And I looked, and behold a pale horse: and his
name that sat on him was Death, and Hell followed
with him. And power was given unto them over the
fourth part of the earth, to kill with the sword,
and with hunger, and with death, and with the
beasts of the earth.

The Revelation of St. John the Divine,
Chapter 6, verse 8

INTRODUCTION

Mainly for the Teacher

This anthology is based upon a selection of war poems that I have used for a sixth-form General Studies course. The original selection, mainly of twentieth-century poems, was restricted in scope because the time available for the course was limited, but in this book I have been able to include a larger number of poems and to extend the selection, so that war poetry from the fourteenth century to the present day is represented. The choice of poetry for any anthology is bound to seem arbitrary, and, especially when a particular theme is chosen, there will be disapproval at the inclusion of one poem because it is hackneyed and another because it is second rate, as there will be indignation at the omission of this poem or that because it is far superior to anything that has been given a place. To try to justify the omissions would be pointless, for this collection pretends to be neither comprehensive nor completely representative, but it may perhaps be desirable to offer some account of why these poems have been selected, of the choice of subject-matter that provides the common theme, and of the purpose I hope this book will serve.

Since my original course was not of a specialist nature, but was intended for sixth-form students, some of whom were studying the arts and some the sciences, I wanted to choose poems with as wide a range of appeal as possible so that a varied selection of poems could be introduced to young people without assuming any previous experience of the serious study of poetry, and discussed at a reasonably adult level. For this reason, too, I have supplied glosses and footnotes, as well as brief explanatory material in the introductions and commentaries accompanying some of the poems, where these might be of help to the

1

non-specialist reader. The nucleus of some twenty poems with which I began served this purpose with moderate success, but I believe that the enlargement of the material undertaken in this book should provide a more satisfactory means of achieving this end simply because there are more poems to choose from. Some justification of the individual poems may be apparent in the commentaries.

The subject of war was chosen because it was desirable to have a unifying theme in a short and concentrated course and because war is a topic which attracts the interest, and may hold the attention, of young people living in the kind of world with which the twentieth century has confronted them. Perhaps the initial appeal is greater to boys than to girls, but I should expect the responses of girls to the predominantly masculine world with which war poetry is concerned to be of particular interest compared with those of boys.

The purpose of the book, therefore, is to provide a number of poems on a single theme and thereby offer an opportunity to students to read them and to discuss what they read. The process of reading poetry deserves particular attention, and more care than most students are inclined to give unless they are taught something of the technique required, so some instruction in the rudiments of the poet's craft is a necessary preliminary if there is to be any value in the discussion of any poem or group of poems. But while some knowledge of prosody will be desirable, of even greater importance will be the question of the nature of the poetry: what a poet is trying to do, as well as his method of doing it; and some profitable discussion can arise from a consideration of this in relation to the poems in this selection. Here, because of the restricted subject-matter, it is possible to make comparisons between poets writing on a similar theme, and to tackle the problem of value and standards of excellence, for while not all the work included is great poetry, some is unquestionably of outstanding quality. Some of the possible comparisons are suggested in the commentaries; others will come to mind as the poems are read.

Inevitably the question of war itself will arise in any discussion prompted by these poems, and the widely varied attitudes of the poets represented here can provide a useful starting point for the pursuit of the many questions—social, historical, psychological, religious—that young people are concerned to talk about in connection with this subject. Primarily, however, the object of the anthology is to offer material for the discussion of poems: discussion which may perhaps lead to some reflection on poetry; and, if possible, to whet the appetites of a few readers for the other and less martial works of the poets who appear in the following pages.

Mainly for the Student

The twentieth century has been unique in man's martial history not for the number of wars it has witnessed, for there is nothing new about the frequency of human aggression, but because its two major conflicts have been called world wars. The Second World War, in particular, indicated the geographical range of modern war, for it was fought in the Arctic seas, across the Atlantic and Pacific oceans, in the jungles of Burma and the deserts of North Africa, as well as in Europe from the Mediterranean to central Russia. Another twentieth-century feature of war has been the involvement of civilians, not because their country has been invaded by an enemy, but through the development of aerial bombing and long-range missiles, and, again, the Second World War demonstrated very adequately the extension of our capacity for destruction in this direction. The conclusion of that war also brought about the probable end of world wars of the old-fashioned kind, for in 1945 the first atomic bombs were dropped on two Japanese cities, and, as a result, the idea of war on an international, inter-continental scale became something of a totally different nature from anything mankind had ever previously experienced.

Today we live, militarily speaking, in a nightmare world in which the technical jargon speaks of megatons, ICBM's, "overkill", radiation hazards; where the threat of war spreading

catastrophically to millions of people is referred to euphemistic-
ally as "escalation"; and where the outbreak of fighting in some
apparently remote part of the world can give rise to the anxiety
that the consequence might be a global conflagration in the
literal sense.

Now this book is not about history or strategy or pacifism
(although the direct or implicit pacifism of some war poetry is
worth considering): it is a book of poems about war, and the
preceding paragraphs are intended to suggest not only that we
are all cruelly conscious of the subject by the accident of our
having been born into this particular period of human existence,
and are probably more acutely aware of it than human beings
have ever been, but that our position in the second half of the
twentieth century—surely, one hopes, a turning point in man's
attitude to war—gives us a peculiarly advantageous viewpoint
from which to consider man's experience of war as it has been
treated over the past 500 years, not by historians or by soldiers,
but by poets.

You may, therefore, find it of interest to consider initially
what the poets represented in this book thought about war, and
for what purposes they used the subject. Some, like the ballad
writers, are concerned simply to tell a story and to record the
heroism of those who took part in a battle. Some, like Tennyson
and Day Lewis, are relating an actual contemporary event and
have strong feelings about who wins and the issues of right and
wrong involved. Johnson is primarily concerned with moral
questions; Shakespeare's interest may be purely his dramatic
purpose in the creation of his Henry V and Coriolanus. Others are
concerned to protest or to warn, or to establish a point of stability
in an unsettled world, and most of these, as might be expected,
are of our own time. There are many attitudes expressed, and it
may be relevant to examine them and ask what particular cir-
cumstances—personal, social, historical—gave rise to them, and
why they were uttered in the particular language and form in
which we find them.

But however interesting may be the subject-matter of these

poems, there is the much more important question of their being poetry. Most people will agree that there is really no such person as a "war poet": there are just poets who happen to write, among other things, about war. Admittedly there are a few men like Wilfred Owen, all of whose best poetry is concerned with war, but nearly all the poets in this book wrote, or are writing, about many other subjects, and it is for their poetry rather than the accident of their subject-matter that they must be considered and judged.

The business of judging a poem, of criticism, is one which some people are reluctant to undertake, because, they say, a poem should be read and enjoyed (or not), and that is all there is to the matter. It should be emphasized at once that, in the opinion of this editor, poetry is for enjoyment, in spite of the solemnity with which it is frequently discussed—a tone which you may even detect in this book—and it is as a means of encouraging the kind of pleasure that poetry can give that books like this one are published; so that if the poems included here can give pleasure without the intrusion of explanations and commentaries the purpose of the book will have been achieved. But the fact remains that a good deal of poetry, particularly when it is presented to the comparatively inexperienced reader, will not yield its full measure of enjoyment without a certain amount of close and trained observation, and that the more closely and observantly one looks at a poem, the greater will be one's understanding and the deeper one's satisfaction. You will probably have discovered this already in other activities which the complexity of the human mind has devised for our enjoyment, for it is as true of sport as it is of the arts: the spectator who knows the finer points of tennis will enjoy a day at Wimbledon more fully than the one who simply sees a ball being hit hard across a net, just as the person who understands something of the technicalities of music will derive more pleasure from a symphony concert than the one to whom Beethoven is merely a glorious noise. This certainly applies to most poetry, so the time spent in attentive study ought to pay dividends in terms of the richer satisfaction which accrues as a result.

The intelligent criticism of a poem depends, first of all, on very careful reading of the piece under consideration. It needs to be read and re-read until one knows what the writer is actually saying: that is, the literal meaning of the words he is using. It is very easy to misread a poem if it is given no more than a superficial glance, and most poetry worth studying deserves more attention than one would give to a newspaper column or the pages of a popular novel. This is not intended as a slight upon newspapers or popular novels, but is a recognition of the fact that poetry uses language in a particularly concentrated form, and that to read it with understanding requires an appropriate concentration of attention.

Together with a concern for what the writer is saying should go an awareness of the means he is using to say it effectively. Without becoming obsessed with technicalities, one can consider rhyme and metre, variations of rhythm, and, very often of particular importance, the imagery employed, for a poet's use of figures of speech is frequently significant in creating the tone of a poem, and is a major factor in the compression of meaning that the language of many poets contains, particularly when considered not in isolation but with reference to the immediate context or to the poem as a whole.

When read with this kind of attention to detail, and with an attitude which should be receptive and sympathetic at this stage, many poems will be found to possess depths of meaning hitherto unperceived and a richness which will repay the effort of mind required to discover it.

Some may argue that the close scrutiny of a poem is likely to destroy the immediacy of appeal it should make, and complain, with Wordsworth,

> Our meddling intellect
> Mis-shapes the beauteous form of things:—
> We murder to dissect.

This objection is not a valid one because the critical "dissection" of a poem is likely to prove fatal only to poor poetry: good poetry will be enjoyed more fully after it has been subjected to close analysis; and since this anthology contains some very good poems, as well as some less good ones, it might be interesting to see which ones withstand the test of scrutiny and which have their inadequacies revealed in the process. In this way, the value of comparison and contrast as useful tools of criticism can be seen.

The commentaries which follow each of the poems or groups of poems in this book suggest some of the comparisons which can be made, and others may occur to you as you read. Usually, these commentaries are intended to serve as points of departure for discussion and argument about the poem in question, and, except when purely factual information is offered, may be accepted or dismissed as the reader sees fit; but they should not be accepted uncritically or rejected without good reason, for the critical faculty which you are invited to bring to bear on the poems may, with proper modifications, be usefully engaged here, too. Criticism does not mean fault-finding, but the healthy scepticism of an inquiring intellect can be a valuable corrective to the tendency found in some unduly docile students to agree with every opinion they are offered.

I said earlier that poetry is for enjoyment. Having since then given the impression to some readers that poetry is for criticism, I should like to reaffirm my belief that criticism is not, or should not be, an end in itself, but is a means of enabling us to derive greater satisfaction from what we experience in poetry. Perhaps "satisfaction" is a better word to employ than "enjoyment" with its associations of gaiety; for good poetry, with its combination of the sensuous and the intellectual, can satisfy the human mind which is itself composed of these two diverse elements. "Enjoyment", "pleasure", "satisfaction"—each may aptly express the effect that poetry can have on the reader who is prepared and equipped to respond to what the poet has to offer. And in this connection I would strongly recommend the reading of poetry aloud, either to oneself, if circumstances permit, or in a class, provided the initial self-consciousness with which some are afflicted can be overcome. The vigour of language and rhythms can be made much more apparent, and the intention of the poet can often become clearer, if this method of communication is adopted.

The satisfaction to be derived from the sensuous element in poetry comes from the almost physical excitement of rhythmical language; the intellectual satisfaction can come from the thought contained in the poem, when we recognize an attitude of mind which is new to us or causes us to see things in a new way; and in an anthology of war poetry this aspect may seem the more important. War has exercised men's minds, as well as maimed their bodies, for a very long time, and the varied responses to war and violence of the poets represented here may reflect something of the widely differing attitudes that human beings in general have adopted towards this strange aspect of man's behaviour. The two epigraphs with which this book opens show two extremely diverse points of view. The plain, blunt words of Gascoigne indicate a rejection of the romantic conception of war, a disillusionment with its glories, and this is an attitude which will be recognized—implied or explicitly stated—as it recurs in the course of the book. The verse from the Bible (a book which contains some remarkable war poetry) suggests the dreadful fascination war has had for men, for it evokes very powerfully a sense of the terror of violence and sudden death, and yet thrills with the excitement of destruction which we seem at times unable to resist.

The passage from Chaucer with which the main part of the book begins shows us a medieval picture of the violence inflicted upon a suffering humanity, attributable to the malign influence of Mars, god of War. Perhaps it is of some significance in the development of man's attitude to war that the concluding poem in the book ends with the simple statement,

I am the one responsible.

GEOFFREY CHAUCER (1340–1400)

THE TEMPLE OF MARS
(From *The Knight's Tale*)

The Knight's Tale, the first of *The Canterbury Tales*, tells the story of two young Theban knights, Palamon and Arcite, who are rivals for the love of Emilia, sister-in-law of their enemy, Theseus. Towards the end of the story, Theseus takes pity on the plight of the rivals and arranges a great tournament in which the two lovers, each with one hundred chosen warriors, will fight for the hand of Emilia. For this purpose he orders the construction of a walled arena, one mile in circumference, and over each of the three gates he builds a temple, one dedicated to Venus, goddess of Love, one to Mars, god of War, and one to Diana, goddess of Chastity. Before the battle, Palamon prays to Venus, Arcite to Mars and Emilia to Diana, and each has his prayer answered—although not in every case quite as the worshipper expects. The three temples are described at some length in the Tale, the most dramatic and lavish being the following account of the Temple of Mars.

> WHY sholde I noght as wel eek[1] telle yow al
> The portreiture that was upon the wal
> Withinne the temple of myghty Mars the rede?
> Al peynted was the wal, in lengthe and brede,
> Lyk to the estres[2] of the grisly place
> That highte[3] the grete temple of Mars in Trace,[4]
> In thilke[5] colde, frosty regioun
> Ther as[6] Mars hath his sovereyn mansioun.

---

[1]*also*   [2]*interior*   [3]*is called*   [4]*Thrace*   [5]*that same*   [6]*where*

First on the wal was peynted a forest,
10   In which ther dwelleth neither man ne best,
With knotty, knarry,[7] bareyne trees olde
Of stubbes[8] sharpe and hidouse to biholde,
In which ther ran a rumbel in a swough,[9]
As though a storm sholde bresten[10] every bough.
And dounward from an hille, under a bente,[11]
Ther stood the temple of Mars armypotente,[12]
Wroght al of burned steel, of which the entree[13]
Was long and streit,[14] and gastly[15] for to see.
And therout came a rage and swich a veze[16]
20   That it made al the gate for to rese.[17]
The northren lyght in at the dores shoon,
For wyndowe on the wal ne was ther noon,
Thurgh which men myghten any light discerne.
The dore was al of adamant eterne,
Yclenched overthwart and endelong[18]
With iren tough; and for to make it strong,
Every pyler, the temple to sustene,
Was tonne greet,[19] of iren bright and shene.
Ther saugh I first the derke ymaginyng[20]
30   Of Felonye, and al the compassyng;[21]
The crueel Ire, reed as any gleede;[22]
The pykepurs,[23] and eek the pale Drede;
The smylere with the knyf under the cloke;
The shepne[24] brennynge[25] with the blake smoke;
The tresoun of the mordrynge[26] in the bedde;
The open werre, with woundes al bibledde;[27]
Contek,[28] with blody knyf and sharp manace.
Al ful of chirkyng[29] was that sory place.
The sleere of hymself yet saugh I ther,—

---

[7]gnarled   [8]stumps   [9]a rushing rumbling noise   [10]break   [11]grassy slope
[12]mighty in arms   [13]entrance   [14]narrow   [15]terrible   [16]such a fierce blast
[17]shake   [18]riveted across and lengthways   [19]thick as a barrel   [20]plotting
[21]way it was accomplished   [22]glowing coal   [23]pick-purse   [24]stable
[25]burning   [26]murdering   [27]covered in blood   [28]strife   [29]strident noises

40   His herte-blood hath bathed al his heer;
The nayl ydryven in the shode[30] a-nyght;
The colde deeth, with mouth gapyng upright.[31]
Amyddes of the temple sat Meschaunce,
With disconfort and sory contenaunce.
Yet saugh I Woodnesse,[32] laughynge in his rage,
Armed Compleint,[33] Outhees,[34] and fiers Outrage;[35]
The careyne[36] in the busk, with throte ycorve;[37]
A thousand slayn, and nat of qualm ystorve;[38]
The tiraunt, with the pray by force yraft;[39]

50   The toun destroyed, ther was no thyng laft.
Yet saugh I brent[40] the shippes hoppesteres;[41]
The hunte[42] strangled with[43] the wilde beres;
The sowe freten[44] the child right in the cradel;
The cook yscalded, for al his longe ladel.
Noght was foryeten[45] by the infortune of Marte:
The cartere[46] overryden with his carte,
Under the wheel ful lowe he lay adoun.
Ther were also, of Martes divisioun,
The barbour, and the bocher,[47] and the smyth,

60   That forgeth sharpe swerdes on his styth.[48]
And al above, depeynted in a tour,
Saugh I Conquest, sittynge in greet honour,
With the sharpe swerd over his heed
Hangynge by a soutil[49] twynes threed. . . . . .
    The statue of Mars upon a carte[50] stood
Armed, and looked grym as he were wood[51]. . . .
A wolf ther stood biforn hym at his feet
With eyen rede, and of a man he eet;
With soutil pencel[52] depeynted was this storie

70   In redoutynge[53] of Mars and of his glorie.

---

[30]*temple*   [31]*lying stretched out with his mouth wide open*   [32]*Madness*
[33]*Discontent*   [34]*Outcry*   [35]*Cruelty*   [36]*corpse*   [37]*cut*
[38]*not dead of the plague*   [39]*seized*   [40]*on fire*   [41]*dancing*   [42]*huntsman*
[43]*by*   [44]*devouring*   [45]*forgotten*   [46]*charioteer*   [47]*butcher*   [48]*anvil*
[49]*thin*   [50]*chariot*   [51]*mad*   [52]*brush*   [53]*reverence*

This is a medieval account of war and violence, but Chaucer's approach to the subject, with its implicit humanity, has a timeless quality which is strikingly modern in its attitude.

The first 28 lines of the passage are notable for the powerful sense of desolation, combined with a feeling of physical harshness and ugliness, conveyed in the description of the temple's appearance. (The two-dimensional "portreiture that was upon the wal Withinne the temple" immediately becomes a three-dimensional reality—a characteristic piece of Chaucerian sleight-of-hand.) The "knotty, knarry, bareyne trees olde Of stubbes sharpe", and the door "Yclenched overthwart and endelong With iren tough" are examples of the feeling of uncompromising hardness Chaucer associates with Mars.

The rest of the piece is interesting for its comprehensiveness: Mars, the god of War, is associated (according to astrological belief), not only with the battlefield but with violence, crime and accident in general, and the prevailing impressions are those of fear and cruelty. These are created by a series of vivid eye-witness descriptions in which a significant detail often evokes a more complex picture in the reader's (or listener's) imagination: the most famous line of the passage,

'The smylere with the knyf under the cloke',

says more about treachery in eight words than could many pages from a lesser writer.

We do not know for certain what was Chaucer's personal experience of war and violence, but these lines express an attitude to the subject which, in spite of Chaucer's characteristic air of detachment—or because of it—is unmistakable in its presentation of grim actuality.

ANONYMOUS (15TH–16TH CENTURIES)

TWO BORDER BALLADS

The border ballads were composed in the period from the late Middle Ages up to the eighteenth century by unknown writers, mainly from the Scottish lowlands, whose poems were handed down orally long before they were ever printed. Because of this oral tradition several versions of the ballads exist, and it is impossible to establish beyond doubt what was the "original" wording. The rivalry between the Earl of Douglas and Percy of Northumberland was the raw material for a number of them. *The Battle of Otterburn* is a Scottish account of one of these almost legendary battles, while *The Hunting of the Cheviot* (*Chevy Chase*), of which the latter part is included here, gives an English version of what may have been the same battle. Froissart, in his *Chronicles*, provides a vivid narrative of the battle, based partly on the oral testimony of men who took part in it.

THE BATTLE OF OTTERBURN

1

It FELL about the Lammas tide,[1]
　When the muir[2]-men win[3] their hay,
The doughty Douglas bound him to ride[4]
　Into England, to drive a prey.

2

He chose the Gordons and the Graemes,
　With them the Lindesays, light and gay;
But the Jardines wald not with him ride,
　And they rue it to this day.

---

[1]*1st August*　　[2]*moor-*　　[3]*dry*　　[4]*set out*

3

And he has burnd the dales of Tyne,
    And part of Bambrough shire,
And three good towers on Reidswire fells,
    He left them all on fire.

4

And he marchd up to Newcastle,
    And rode it round about:
"O wha's the lord of this castle?
    Or wha's the lady o't?"

5

But up spake proud lord Percy then,
    And O but he spake hie!
"I am the lord of this castle,
    My wife's the lady gay."

6

"If thou'rt the lord of this castle,
    Sae weel it pleases me,
For, ere I cross the Border fells,
    The tane⁵ of us shall die."

7

He took a lang spear in his hand,
    Shod with the metal free,⁶
And for to meet the Douglas there
    He rode right furiouslie.

8

But O how pale his lady lookd
    Frae aff the castle-wa,
When down before the Scottish spear
    She saw proud Percy fa.

---

⁵*the one*   ⁶*fine*

9

"Had we twa been upon the green,
   And never an eye to see,
I wad hae had you, flesh and fell;[7]
   But your sword sall gae wi me."

10

"But gae ye up to Otterbourne,
   And wait there dayis three,
And, if I come not ere three dayis end,
   A fause knight ca ye me."

11

"The Otterbourne's a bonnie burn;
   'Tis pleasant there to be;
But there is nought at Otterbourne
   To feed my men and me.

12

"The deer rins wild on hill and dale,
   The birds fly wild from tree to tree;
But there is neither bread nor kale[8]
   To fend[9] my men and me.

13

"Yet I will stay at Otterbourne,
   Where you shall welcome be;
And, if ye come not at three dayis end,
   A fause lord I'll ca thee."

14

"Thither will I come," proud Percy said,
   "By the might of Our Ladye;"
"There will I bide thee," said the Douglas,
   "My troth I plight to thee."

---

[7]*skin*   [8]*green-stuff*   [9]*provide for*

15

They lighted high on Otterbourne,
    Upon the bent[10] sae brown;
They lighted high on Otterbourne,
    And threw their pallions[11] down.

16

And he that had a bonnie boy,
    Sent out his horse to grass;
And he that had not a bonnie boy,
    His ain servant he was.

17

But up then spake a little page,
    Before the peep of dawn:
"O waken ye, waken ye, my good lord,
    For Percy's hard at hand."

18

"Ye lie, ye lie, ye liar loud!
    Sae loud I hear ye lie:
For Percy had not men yestreen[12]
    To dight[13] my men and me.

19

"But I have dreamd a dreary dream,
    Beyond the Isle of Sky;
I saw a dead man win a fight,
    And I think that man was I."

20

He belted on his guid braid sword,
    And to the field he ran,
But he forgot the helmet good,
    That should have kept his brain.

---

[10]*coarse grass-land*   [11]*tents*   [12]*last evening*   [13]*beat, deal with*

21

When Percy wi the Douglas met,
  I wat[14] he was fu fain;[15]
They swakked[16] their swords, till sair they swat,[17]
  And the blood ran down like rain.

22

But Percy with his good broad sword,
  That could so sharply wound,
Has wounded Douglas on the brow,
  Till he fell to the ground.

23

Then he calld on his little foot-page,
  And said, "Run speedilie,
And fetch my ain dear sister's son,
  Sir Hugh Montgomery."

24

"My nephew good," the Douglas said,
  "What recks the death of ane!
Last night I dreamd a dreary dream,
  And I ken the day's thy ain.

25

"My wound is deep; I fain would sleep;
  Take thou the vanguard of the three,
And hide me by the braken-bush,
  That grows on yonder lilye lee.[18]

26

"O bury me by the braken-bush,
  Beneath the blooming brier;
Let never living mortal ken
  That ere a kindly[19] Scot lies here."

---

[14]*know*   [15]*very eager*   [16]*clashed*   [17]*sweated*   [18]*lovely place(?)*   [19]*native*

27

He lifted up that noble lord,
    Wi the saut tear in his ee;
He hid him in the braken-bush,
    That his merrie men might not see.

28

The moon was clear, the day drew near,
    The spears in flinders[20] flew,
But mony a gallant Englishman
    Ere day the Scotsmen slew.

29

The Gordons good, in English blood
    They steepd their hose and shoon;
The Lindsays flew like fire about,
    Till all the fray was done.

30

The Percy and Montgomery met,
    That either of other were fain;
They swapped[21] swords and they twa swat,
    And aye the blood ran down between.

31

"Now yield thee, yield thee, Percy," he said,
    "Or else I vow I'll lay thee low!"
"To whom must I yield," quoth Earl Percy,
    "Now that I see it must be so?"

32

"Thou shalt not yield to lord nor loun,[22]
    Nor yet shalt thou yield to me;
But yield thee to the braken-bush,
    That grows upon yon lilye lee."

---

[20]*splinters*   [21]*clashed*   [22]*low-born person*

33

"I will not yield to a braken-bush,
  Nor yet will I yield to a brier;
But I would yield to Earl Douglas,
  Or Sir Hugh the Montgomery, if he were here."

34

As soon as he knew it was Montgomery,
  He struck his sword's point in the gronde;
The Montgomery was a courteous knight,
  And quickly took him by the honde.

35

This deed was done at the Otterbourne,
  About the breaking of the day;
Earl Douglas was buried at the braken-bush,
  And the Percy led captive away.

From THE HUNTING OF THE CHEVIOT
(CHEVY CHASE)

(The first part of the ballad tells how Percy and his followers went hunting in the Cheviot hills in defiance of the Douglas, whose territory it was. Douglas and his men arrive, and after a challenge to single combat from Douglas, which Percy refuses because his men will not see him fight alone, the battle begins.)

1

THE Englishmen had their bows ybent,
  Their hearts were good ynoughe;
The first of arrows that they shot off,
  Seven score spearmen they sloughe.[1]

---

[1] *slew*

2

Yet bides the Earl Douglas upon the bent,
    A captain good ynoughe;
And that was sene verament,[2]
    For he wrought them both woe and wouche.[3]

3

The Douglas parted his host in three,
    Like a cheffe chieftain of pride;
With sure spears of mighty tree,
    They come in on every side.

4

Thrughe our English archery
    Gave many a wound full wide;
Many a doughty[4] they gar'd[5] to die,
    Which gained them no pride.

5

The Englishmen let their bows be,
    And pulde out brands[6] that were bright;
It was a heavy sight to see
    Bright swords on basnets[7] light.

6

Thorowe rich mail and manoplie[8]
    Many stern[9] they struck down straight;
Many a freyke[10] that was full free[11]
    There under foot did light.

7

At last the Douglas and the Percy met,
    Like to captains of might and main;
They swapt[12] together till they both swat,
    With swords that were of fine Milaine.

---

[2]*truly*   [3]*harm, evil*   [4]*brave man*   [5]*caused*   [6]*swords*   [7]*helmets*
[8]*gauntlet*   [9]*stern men, warriors*   [10]*bold fellow;*   [11]*brave*   [12]*exchanged blows*

8

These worthy freykes for to fight
   Thereto they were full fain,
Till the blood out of their basnets sprent,[13]
   As ever did hail or rain.

9

"Yield thee, Percy," said the Douglas,
   "And i' faith I shall thee bring
Where thou shalt have an earl's wages
   Of Jamie our Scottish king.

10

Thou shalt have thy ransom free,
   I hight[14] thee here this thing;
For the manfullest man yet art thou
   That ever I conquered in field fighting."

11

"Nay," said the lord Percy,
   "I told it thee beforn,
That I would never yielded be
   To no man of a woman born."

12

With that there came an arrow hastely,
   Forth of a mighty wane;[15]
It hath stricken the Earl Douglas
   In at the breast-bane.

13

Thorowe liver and lunges both
   The sharp arrow is gane,
That never after in all his life-days
   He spake mo words but ane:
That was, "Fight ye, my merry men, whiles ye may,
   For my life-days ben gane."

---

[13]*spurted*   [14]*promise*   [15]*host, multitude*

14

The Percy leaned on his brand,
    And saw the Douglas dee;
He took the dead man by the hand,
    And said, "Woe is me for thee!

15

To have saved thy life I would have parted with
    My lands for yeares three,
For a better man, of heart nor of hand
    Was not in all the north countrye."

16

Of all that saw a Scottish knight,
    Was called Sir Hugh the Montgomery;
He saw the Douglas to the death was dight,[16]
    He spended[17] a spear, a trusty tree.[18]

17

He rode upon a corsiare[19]
    Through a hundred archery:
He never stinted,[20] nor never blane,[21]
    Till he came to the good lord Percy.

18

He set upon the lord Percy
    A dint[22] that was full sore;
With a sure spear of a mighty tree
    Clean thorowe the body he the Percy bore,

19

At the other side that a man might see
    A large cloth-yard and more:
Two better captains were not in Cristianty
    Than that day slain were there.

---

[16]*done*   [17]*got ready*   [18]*of trusty wood*   [19]*courser, charger*   [20]*stopped*
[21]*ceased*   [22]*blow*

20

An archer of Northumberland
  Saw slain was the lord Percy;
He bar a bent bow in his hand,
  Was made of a trusty tree.

21

An arrow that a cloth-yard was lang
  To the hard steel haled[23] he;
A dint that was both sad[24] and sore
  He set on Sir Hugh the Montgomery.

22

The dint it was both sad and sore
  That he on Montgomery set;
The swan-feathers that his arrow bore
  With his heart-blood they were wet.

23

There was never a freyke one foot would flee,
  But still in stour[25] did stand;
Hewing on each other while they might dree,[26]
  With many a baleful brand.

24

This battle began in Cheviot
  An hour before the noon,
And when the evensong bell was rung,
  The battle was not half done.

25

They took their stand on either hand
  By the light of the moon;
Many had no strength for to stand
  In Cheviot the hills abon.

---

[23]pulled   [24]heavy   [25]tumult of battle   [26]endure

26

Of fifteen hundred archers of England
   Went away but seventy and three;
Of twenty hundred spearmen of Scotland,
   But even five and fifty.

27

But all were slain Cheviot within;
   They had no strength to stand on hie;
The child may rue that is unborn,
   It was the more pity.

28

There was slain, with the lord Percy,
   Sir John of Agerstone,
Sir Roger, the hinde[27] Hartly,
   Sir William, the bold Hearone.

29

Sir George, the worthy Lumley,
   A knight of great renown,
Sir Ralph, the rich Rugbe,
   With dints were beaten down.

30

For Witherington my heart was woe,
   That ever he slain should be;
For when both his legs were hewn in two,
   Yet he kneeled and fought on his knee.

31

There was slain, with the doughty Douglas,
   Sir Hugh the Montgomery,
Sir Davy Lambwell, that worthy was,
   His sister's son was he.

---

[27]*courteous*

32

Sir Charles a Murray in that place,
    That never a foot would flee;
Sir Hugh Maxwell, a lord he was,
    With the Douglas did he dee.

33

So on the morrow they made them biers
    Of birch and hazel so gray;
Many widows, with weeping tears,
    Came to fetch their makes[28] away.

34

Teviotdale may carp[29] of care,
    Northumberland may make great moan,
For two such captains as slain were there
    On the March-parts shall never be none.

35

Word is come to Edinboro',
    To Jamie the Scottish king,
That doughty Douglas, lieutenant of the Marches,
    He lay slain Cheviot within.

36

His hands did he weal[30] and wring,
    He said, "Alas, and woe is me!
Such another captain Scotland within",
    He said, "i'faith shall never be."

37

Word is come to lovely London,
    Till the fourth Harry our king,
That lord Percy, lieutenant of the Marches,
    He lay slain Cheviot within.

---

[28]*mates, husbands*   [29]*talk*   [30]*clench*

38

"God have mercy on his soul," said King Harry,
    "Good Lord, if thy will it be!
I have a hundred captains in England," he said,
    "As good as ever was he:
But, Percy, an I brook[31] my life,
    Thy death well quit[32] shall be."

39

As our noble king made his avow,
    Like a noble prince of renown,
For the death of the lord Percy
    He did the battle of Homble-down;

40

Where six and thirty Scottish knights
    On a day were beaten down;
Glendale glittered on their armour bright,
    Over castle, tower and town.

41

This was the hunting of the Cheviot,
    That e'er began this spurn![33]
Old men that know the ground well ynough
    Call it the battle of Otterburn.

42

At Otterburn began this spurn,
    Upon a Monanday;
There was the doughty Douglas slain,
    The Percy never went away.

43

There was never a time on the March-parts
    Since the Douglas and the Percy met,
But it is marvel an the red blood ran not
    As the reane does in the street.[34]

---

[31]*possess, enjoy*   [32]*avenged*   [33]*battle, encounter(?)*   [34]*gutter*

44

Jesu Christ our bales[35] bete,[36]
And to the bliss us bring!
Thus was the hunting of the Cheviot:
God send us all good ending!

Ballads were intended to be sung—a fact that is often forgotten when we read them in books—and these two border ballads were probably in the repertoire of Tudor minstrels.

In some ways their subject-matter reminds us of something more recent and familiar: the American wild west with its feuds and rivalries, its territorial jealousies and lawless violence; and it is interesting to note that versions of some of these ballads, suitably adapted, have survived into modern times in the remoter parts of the United States.

The main characteristics of ballads such as *The Battle of Otterburn* and *Chevy Chase* are the directness and economy with which their stories are told, and the impersonal tone of the narrator, who keeps well in the background.

The directness of the story-telling can be illustrated from the beginning of *The Battle of Otterburn*. In stanza 3, the Douglas is already rampaging through Northumberland, and in stanza 4 he is challenging Percy in Newcastle. The dialogue between the two rivals is presented almost abruptly, and the sense of an impending clash between powerful and proud adversaries is created without waste of words. Another characteristic piece of terseness is shown in stanza 16.

The second part of *Chevy Chase* begins with similar economy: a hail of arrows falls upon the Scottish spearmen, but Douglas patiently waits for the right moment to launch his three-fold attack upon the enemy, who now draw their swords for hand-to-hand fighting.

There is very rarely any comment from the narrator on the events described, unless such comment helps to convey a clearer

---

[35]*woes*   [36]*relieve*

impression of the action. The most violent episodes in both poems
exhibit this impersonal tone:

> They swakked their swords till sair they swat,
> And the blood ran down like rain

and

> The Gordons good, in English blood,
> They steepd their hose and shoon

in *The Battle of Otterburn;*

> Thorowe liver and lunges both
> The sharp arrow is gane

and the gruesomeness of Witherington's courage—

> For when both his legs were hewn in two
> Yet he kneeled and fought on his knee

in *Chevy Chase*, all describe bloodshed and mutilation, but with no
attempt to sensationalize, moralize or present anything but the
stark facts.

This is not to say that there is no feeling in these ballads; the
feeling arises not from sophisticated devices or from the intrusion
of the story-teller, but from the sheer vigour and pace of the
verse and from uncomplicated emotions such as admiration for
courage and loyalty. Warfare in these ballads is seen as something
heroic: in the mutual respect for each other's qualities shown by
Percy and Douglas; in the heroism of Douglas in his wish to be
buried in the bracken bush so that his loss will not sap the morale
of his men; and in the grim sense of loyalty that sets up a chain of
revenge as Montgomery requites the death of Douglas and the
Northumberland archer slays Montgomery. We may regard the
feelings expressed as barbaric, but they faithfully and dramatic-
ally convey the barbarity of these savage encounters, in verse that
is refreshing in its rough, unsophisticated straightforwardness.

WILLIAM SHAKESPEARE (1564–1616)

KING HENRY V
(Parts of Act III)

King Henry V has invaded France, determined to win the
territories he claims are his. The English are now laying siege to
the town of Harfleur, and in Scene 1 the King calls upon his men
to fight hard to bring about its surrender. Scene 2, a part of
which is given here, begins with a mocking echo of the King's
speech from the loud-mouthed Bardolph.

SCENE 1

KING HENRY: Once more unto the breach, dear friends,
    once more;
    Or close the wall up with our English dead.
    In peace there's nothing so becomes a man
    As modest stillness and humility:
    But when the blast of war blows in our ears,
    Then imitate the action of the tiger;
    Stiffen the sinews, summon up the blood,
    Disguise fair nature with hard-favour'd rage;
    Then lend the eye a terrible aspect;
10   Let it pry through the portage[1] of the head
    Like the brass cannon; let the brow o'erwhelm it
    As fearfully as doth a galled[2] rock
    O'erhang and jutty[3] his confounded base,
    Swill'd with the wild and wasteful ocean.
    Now set the teeth and stretch the nostril wide,
    Hold hard the breath and bend up every spirit

---

[1]*porthole* [2]*worn away* [3]*project beyond*

To his full height. On, on, you noblest English,
Whose blood is fet[4] from fathers of war-proof ![5]
Fathers that, like so many Alexanders,
Have in these parts from morn till even fought,
And sheathed their swords for lack of argu-
ment:[6]
Dishonour not your mothers; now attest
That those whom you call'd fathers did beget
you.
Be copy now to men of grosser blood,
And teach them how to war. And you, good
yeomen,
Whose limbs were made in England, show us
here
The mettle[7] of your pasture; let us swear
That you are worth your breeding; which I
doubt not;
For there is none of you so mean and base,
That hath not noble lustre in your eyes.
I see you stand like greyhounds in the slips,[8]
Straining upon the start. The game's afoot:
Follow your spirit, and upon this charge
Cry "God for Harry, England, and
Saint George!"

SCENE 2

Enter Nym, Bardolph, Pistol and Boy

BARDOLPH: On, on, on, on, on! to the breach, to the breach!

NYM: Pray thee, corporal, stay: the knocks are too hot; and, for mine own part, I have not a case[9] of lives: the humour of it is too hot, that is the very plain-song of it.[10]

---

[4]*derived*   [5]*tested in war*   [6]*reason for fighting*   [7]*quality*   [8]*leash*
[9]*set*   [10]*the matter put simply*

PISTOL: The plain-song is most just; for humours do abound:
Knocks go and come; God's vassals drop and die;
                    And sword and shield,
                    In bloody field,
                    Doth win immortal fame.

BOY: Would I were in an alehouse in London! I would give all
my fame for a pot of ale and safety. . . .

SCENE 3

The Governor of Harfleur appears on the walls of the town and is
addressed by King Henry, who demands his surrender and warns him of
the terrible consequences if he refuses.

KING HENRY: How yet resolves the governor of the town?
                    This is the latest parle[11] we will admit:
                    Therefore to our best mercy give yourselves;
                    Or like to men proud of destruction
                    Defy us to our worst: for, as I am a soldier,
                    A name that in my thoughts becomes me best,
                    If I begin the battery once again,
                    I will not leave the half-achieved Harfleur
                    Till in her ashes she lies buried.
10   The gates of mercy shall be all shut up,
                    And the flesh'd[12] soldier, rough and hard of
                         heart,
                    In liberty of bloody hand shall range
                    With conscience wide as hell, mowing like grass
                    Your fresh-fair virgins and your flowering infants.
                    What is it then to me, if impious war,
                    Array'd in flames like to the prince of fiends,
                    Do, with his smirch'd complexion, all fell[13] feats
                    Enlink'd to waste and desolation?
                    What is't to me, when you yourselves are cause,

---

[11]*parley*   [12]*hardened in bloodshed*   [13]*cruel*

20 If your pure maidens fall into the hand
Of hot and forcing violation?
What rein can hold licentious wickedness
When down the hill he holds his fierce career?[14]
We may as bootless[15] spend our vain command
Upon the enraged soldiers in their spoil
As send precepts to the leviathan[16]
To come ashore. Therefore, you men of Harfleur,
Take pity of your town and of your people,
Whiles yet my soldiers are in my command;
30 Whiles yet the cool and temperate wind of grace
O'erblows the filthy and contagious clouds
Of heady murder, spoil and villany.
If not, why, in a moment look to see
The blind and bloody soldier with foul hand
Defile the locks of your shrill-shrieking daughters;
Your fathers taken by the silver beards,
And their most reverend heads dash'd to the
walls,
Your naked infants spitted upon pikes,
Whiles the mad mothers with their howls
confus'd
40 Do break the clouds, as did the wives of Jewry
At Herod's bloody-hunting slaughtermen.
What say you? will you yield, and this avoid,
Or, guilty in defence, be thus destroy'd?

GOVERNOR: Our expectation hath this day an end:
The Dauphin, whom of succours we entreated,
Returns us that his powers are yet not ready
To raise so great a siege. Therefore, great king,
We yield our town and lives to thy soft mercy.
Enter our gates; dispose of us and ours;
50 For we no longer are defensible.

---

[14]*gallop*   [15]*uselessly*   [16]*sea monster*

The main impression Shakespeare's *Henry V* makes upon an audience is one of patriotic excitement. The story of the play, told with eloquent rhetoric, is of an ideal English king who fights a just war against an enemy whose forces far outnumber his, and who emerges from it triumphant but humble.

Patriotic feeling is certainly a major theme in the play, and it reflects the fervent nationalism of the first Elizabethan age; but a closer examination suggests that Shakespeare was not content with simple jingoism, and that he introduced other, more realistic elements into the play which perhaps cast a shadow over the bright glitter of royal heroics.

The first of these extracts from Act III illustrates this point, for in the course of this very famous patriotic speech the King instructs his men to put aside their humanity in order to become efficient fighting animals: the detailed directions on how to create a war-like facial expression—sinews, eye, brow, teeth and nostrils —are calculated to produce the appearance of a savage beast, and "fair nature" is very effectively disguised. (Try it for yourself—preferably when no-one is looking.)

At the beginning of the second scene there is a deliberate piece of "debunking" by Shakespeare when he shows us how the ordinary disreputable soldier reacts to the King's call to action. Although this is not sufficiently significant to dim Henry's glory in the play as a whole, it does, in its context, give us a more down-to-earth view of the situation. Bardolph's cynical mimicry, Nym's timidity, Pistol's pretentiousness and the Boy's homesickness are as much a part of war as the valour of the yeomen of England.

King Henry's speech in Scene 3 is another example of the way Shakespeare shows us the ugliness of warfare as it was known at the end of the sixteenth century. In calling for the surrender of Harfleur the King threatens the Governor with every kind of atrocity if he will not submit, and emphasis is given to the threat not only by the violence of the language and the rhetorical flow of the verse, but by the insistent repetition of the outrages to be committed. The rape and slaughter of the defenceless are prevented by the Governor's decision to yield, but the old, the women and the children are seen as legitimate victims of war—as they were to be in Guernica, Coventry, Dresden and Hiroshima.

CORIOLANUS

(Part of Act II, Scene 2)

Caius Marcius, a Roman general, has recently inflicted a humiliating defeat upon the Volsces by capturing their city of Corioli. On his return in triumph to Rome he is given the name Coriolanus in honour of his victory. There is now a proposal to make him Consul, but because of his open and bitter contempt for the common people there is strong opposition to this suggestion. In this speech Cominius, a friend of Coriolanus and a fellow general, addresses the rulers of Rome and tells them of Coriolanus' outstanding qualities in war.

COMINIUS: The deeds of Coriolanus
            Should not be utter'd feebly. It is held
            That valour is the chiefest virtue and
            Most dignifies the haver: if it be,
            The man I speak of cannot in the world
            Be singly counterpoised.[1] At sixteen years,
            When Tarquin made a head for[2] Rome, he fought
            Beyond the mark[3] of others; our then dictator
            Whom with all praise I point at, saw him fight,
10   When with his Amazonian[4] chin he drove
            The bristled lips before him: he bestrid
            An o'er-press'd Roman, and i' the consul's view
            Slew three opposers: Tarquin's self he met,
            And struck him on his knee: in that day's feats,

---

[1]equalled   [2]raised an army against   [3]power   [4]beardless

When he might act the woman in the scene,
He prov'd best man i' the field, and for his meed[5]
Was brow-bound with the oak. His pupil age[6]
Man-enter'd[7] thus, he waxed like a sea;
And, in the brunt of seventeen battles since,
20   He lurch'd[8] all swords of the garland. For this last
Before and in Corioli, let me say,
I cannot speak him home:[9] he stopp'd the fliers;
And by his rare example made the coward
Turn terror into sport: as weeds before
A vessel under sail, so men obey'd,
And fell below his stem: his sword, death's stamp,
Where it did mark, it took;[10] from face to foot
He was a thing of blood, whose every motion
Was timed with dying cries: alone he enter'd
30   The mortal[11] gate of the city, which he painted
With shunless destiny; aidless came off,[12]
And with a sudden re-enforcement struck
Corioli like a planet.[13] now all's his:
When, by and by, the din of war gan pierce
His ready sense; then straight his doubled spirit
Requicken'd what in flesh was fatigate,[14]
And to the battle came he; where he did
Run reeking o'er the lives of men, as if
'Twere a perpetual spoil: and till we call'd
40   Both field and city ours, he never stood
To ease his breast with panting. . . .
                Our spoils he kick'd at,[15]
And look'd upon things precious, as they were
The common muck of the world: he covets less
Than misery itself would give; rewards
His deeds with doing them, and is content
To spend the time[16] to end it.

---

[5]*reward*   [6]*boyhood*   [7]*initiated into manhood*   [8]*robbed*   [9]*adequately praise him*
[10]*took effect*   [11]*fatal*   [12]*escaped*   [13]*with disaster*   [14]*fatigued*
[15]*scorned*   [16]*the present moment*

Many of Shakespeare's most important characters were soldiers—"A name that in my thoughts becomes me best," says King Henry V—and military themes appear in many of the plays. Apart from the principals in the English history plays there were Julius Caesar and Mark Antony, Othello and Macbeth, while at Hamlet's death Fortinbras ordered

> The soldiers' music and the rites of war.

Of all Shakespeare's soldiers, Coriolanus, whose mother, Volumnia, "was pleased to let him seek danger where he was like to find fame", is probably the most uncompromising in his dedication to the military life, going to battle

> Like to a harvest man that's task'd to mow
> Or all, or lose his hire,

as Cominius portrays him in this speech.

But Cominius, too, is a soldier, and Shakespeare makes this clear in the words he gives him. Not only does Cominius show his unstinted and professional admiration for Coriolanus' deeds, but the very tone of the speech is that of the commander of armies. Sometimes within the rhythm of the blank verse line and sometimes running athwart it can be heard the clipped accents of the general. The blunt vigour of the speech is reinforced by the frequent use of harsh-sounding words, especially those with hard consonantal sounds, such as "bristled", "struck", "brunt", "lurch'd", "stamp", "mark", "fatigate", "kick'd at" and "muck"; and by such vivid phrases as "whose every motion Was timed with dying cries"; "with shunless destiny" and "run reeking o'er the lives of men", the concentrated meaning of which seems to explode and illuminate the context like a star-shell.

Cominius' speech has nothing explicit to say about war in general: he is concerned only with the exploits of one warrior whose attitude and actions he accepts without question; and he puts on record the feats of a soldier whose single-minded devotion to war is skilfully reflected in the muscular tautness of the language in which it is described.

JOHN MILTON (1608–1674)

WAR IN HEAVEN

(From *Paradise Lost*, Book VI)

Milton's *Paradise Lost* tells in the course of its twelve books the story of Man's disobedience in the Garden of Eden and his consequent loss of Paradise, brought about by the corrupting influence of Satan who rebelled against God in Heaven and was cast out with his followers to Hell. In Book VI the archangel Raphael is in the course of giving Adam and Eve an account of Satan's rebellion and how it was crushed by God and by His Son.

In the first of the following extracts Raphael tells how God sent Michael and Gabriel to lead Heaven's armies against Satan; in the second he reaches the climax of the account when he describes how, on the third day of the war, the Son of God is sent out alone in God's own chariot, drawn by "four cherubic Shapes", to bring destruction upon Satan and his forces and drive them out of Heaven to the place of punishment prepared for them.

> So SPAKE the Sovran Voice; and clouds began
> To darken all the hill, and smoke to roll
> In dusky wreaths reluctant flames, the sign
> Of wrath awaked; nor with less dread the loud
> Ethereal trumpet from on high gan blow.
> At which command the Powers Militant
> That stood for Heaven, in mighty quadrate joined
> Of union irresistible, moved on
> In silence their bright legions to the sound
10 Of instrumental harmony, that breathed
> Heroic ardour to adventurous deeds
> Under their godlike leaders, in the cause
> Of God and his Messiah. On they move,

Indissolubly firm; nor obvious[1] hill,
Nor straitening vale, nor wood, nor stream, divides
Their perfect ranks; for high above the ground
Their march was, and the passive air upbore
Their nimble tread. As when the total kind
Of birds, in orderly array on wing,
20   Came summoned over Eden to receive
Their names of thee; so over many a tract
Of Heaven they marched, and many a province wide,
Tenfold the length of this terrene. At last
Far in the horizon, to the north, appeared
From skirt to skirt a fiery region, stretched
In battailous aspect; and, nearer view,
Bristled with upright beams innumerable
Of rigid spears, and helmets thronged, and shields
Various, with boastful argument portrayed,[2]
30   The banded powers of Satan hasting on
With furious expedition; for they weened[3]
That self-same day, by fight or by surprise,
To win the Mount of God, and on his Throne
To set the envier of his state, the proud
Aspirer.

So spake the Son, and into terror changed
His countenance, too severe to be beheld,
And full of wrath bent on his enemies.
At once the Four spread out their starry wings
With dreadful shade contiguous, and the orbs
Of his fierce chariot rolled, as with the sound
Of torrent floods, or of a numerous host.
He on his impious foes right onward drove,
Gloomy as Night. Under his burning wheels
10   The steadfast Empyrean shook throughout,
All but the throne itself of God. Full soon

---

[1]*obstructive*   [2]*painted*   [3]*expected*

Among them he arrived, in his right hand
Grasping ten thousand thunders, which he sent
Before him, such as in their souls infixed
Plagues. They, astonished,[4] all resistance lost,
All courage; down their idle weapons dropt;
O'er shields, and helms, and helmed heads he rode
Of Thrones and mighty Seraphim prostrate,
That wished the mountains now might be again
20   Thrown on them, as a shelter from his ire.
Nor less on either side tempestuous fell
His arrows, from the fourfold-visaged Four,
Distinct[5] with eyes, and from the living wheels,
Distinct alike with multitude of eyes;
One spirit in them ruled, and every eye
Glared lightning, and shot forth pernicious fire
Among the accursed, that withered all their strength,
And of their wonted vigour left them drained,
Exhausted, spiritless, afflicted, fallen.
30   Yet half his strength he put not forth, but checked
His thunder in mid-volley; for he meant
Not to destroy, but root them out of Heaven.
The overthrown he raised, and, as a herd
Of goats or timorous flock together thronged,
Drove them before him thunderstruck, pursued
With terrors and with furies to the bounds
And crystal wall of Heaven; which, opening wide,
Rolled inward, and a spacious gap disclosed
Into the wasteful Deep. The monstrous sight
40   Strook them with horror backward; but far worse
Urged them behind: headlong themselves they threw
Down from the verge of Heaven: eternal wrath
Burnt after them to the bottomless pit.
Hell heard the unsufferable noise; Hell saw
Heaven ruining from Heaven, and would have fled

---

[4] *thunderstruck*   [5] *adorned*

> Affrighted; but strict Fate had cast too deep
> Her dark foundations, and too fast had bound.
> Nine days they fell; confounded Chaos roared,
> And felt tenfold confusion in their fall
> 50   Through his wild Anarchy; so huge a rout
> Encumbered him with ruin. Hell at last,
> Yawning, received them whole, and on them closed—
> Hell, their fit habitation, fraught with fire
> Unquenchable, the house of woe and pain.

Perhaps some justification is required for the inclusion of these extracts, since the battles described in Book VI of *Paradise Lost* are unknown to history and were fought, as far as we know, only in Milton's imagination. But they represent a notable attempt to portray in blank verse a cosmic war waged by supernatural beings as if in fact that war took place, rather than as if it were merely allegorical, in the manner of Spenser or Bunyan. They are therefore examples of "war poetry", although of a rather special kind.

One of Milton's problems in *Paradise Lost* was that of conveying to the reader a sense of scale, for his scene was the Universe, his characters included Almighty God and his adversary, Satan. To some extent the problem was solved by the language he invented for the poem: English overlaid with Latin constructions and vocabulary; a majestic use of proper nouns; and, closely connected with the language, by the use he made of the blank verse line with its sonorous roll and expansiveness, quite unlike the blank verse of any other writer in English. (Compare the Shakespeare and Cowper extracts elsewhere in this anthology.)

Both these factors can be illustrated from the passages quoted here. The first of them demonstrates Milton's remarkable skill in managing the blank verse line in order to create the impression of perfect control exercised over vast forces. From line 4 there is the measured movement of a powerful army advancing as one unit; from line 9, music is added to the effect, reinforcing the impression of "harmony"; and as the verse moves on there is a sense of gathering momentum, the army surging forward without resistance. In the sixteenth line there is a lifting movement, accompanied by a sense of lightness as we are told of their march above the ground, and this effect is sustained by the simile beginning in line 18. From line 23 we leave the forces of Gabriel and Michael and look towards the distant horizon at the hosts of Satan, and here the more agitated movement of the verse seems to suggest in contrast a sense of disharmony and a hectic haste.

The second extract, which describes the climax of the war, conveys, in Milton's control of the verse, something of the terrible might of the Son of God as he rides inexorably upon the enemy. The first fourteen lines suggest a series of tremendous blows descending on the rebel angels. From "They, astonished" (line 15), the beginning of the rout is discerned: their hopelessness is felt not merely in the words but in the rhythm of the verse. With the rain of deadly arrows falling, the disarray and defeat of the enemy is complete, but the attack continues relentlessly as the long sentence unfolds, the abject condition of the vanquished being reiterated in the four concluding adjectives in line 29. Their final overthrow as they are expelled from Heaven is powerfully described in the last eighteen lines in a succession of abrupt statements which convey not only the horror of their fall, but something of the righteous satisfaction of the narrator (Raphael/ Milton) as the ungodly are thrust with overwhelming fury into the depths of Hell.

The artificially created language and the authoritative sweep of the Miltonic line are admirably suited to the description of such supernatural warfare.

JOHN DRYDEN (1631–1700)

WAR AT SEA

(From *Annus Mirabilis: the Year of Wonders, 1666*)

This poem was written to celebrate some of the events of what at the time seemed a momentous year in English history, and describes a number of naval engagements with the Dutch, and the Great Fire of London.

The following extract tells of the first two days of a four-day battle with the Dutch fleet. Prince Rupert had been ordered to intercept a French fleet, believed to be about to join the Dutch, leaving his co-commander, General Monk (1st Duke of Albermarle) with fifty-four ships to engage a numerically superior enemy off the North Foreland. The battle, fought from 1–4 June 1666, resulted in English losses of twenty ships and 6000 men (including Vice-Admiral Sir William Berkeley); but the Dutch were defeated by Rupert and Albermarle the following month.

1

OUR fleet divides, and straight the Dutch appear,
In number and a famed commander bold:
The narrow seas can scarce their navy bear
Or crowded vessels can their soldiers hold.

2

The Duke, less numerous, but in courage more,
On wings of all the winds to combat flies;
His murdering guns a loud defiance roar,
And bloody crosses on his flag-staffs rise.

3

Both furl their sails and strip them for the fight;
Their folded sheets dismiss the useless air;
The Elean plains* could boast no nobler fight,
When struggling champions did their bodies bare.

4

Borne each by other in a distant line,
The sea-built forts in dreadful order move;
So vast the noise, as if not fleets did join,
But lands unfixed and floating nations strove.

---

* Where the Olympic games were held.

5

Now passed, on either side they nimbly tack;
Both strive to intercept and guide the wind:
And in its eye more closely they come back
To finish all the deaths they left behind.

6

On high-raised decks the haughty Belgians* ride,
Beneath whose shade our humble frigates go;
Such port the elephant bears, and so defied
By the rhinoceros, her unequal foe.

7

And as the build, so different is the fight;
Their mounting shot is on our sails designed:
Deep in their hulls our deadly bullets light
And through the yielding planks a passage find.

8

Our dreaded Admiral from far they threat,
Whose battered rigging their whole war receives;
All bare, like some old oak which tempests beat,
He stands, and sees below his scattered leaves.

9

Heroes of old when wounded shelter sought;
But he, who meets all danger with disdain,
Even in their face his ship to anchor brought
And steeple-high stood propped upon the main.

10

At this excess of courage all-amazed,
The foremost of his foes a while withdrew;
With such respect in entered Rome they gazed
Who on high chairs the god-like fathers saw.†

---

* i.e. the Dutch.

† According to Livy, when the Gauls invaded Rome in 387 B.C. they were
momentarily awe-struck by the sight of the chief citizens sitting robed in their
chairs of state.

11

And now as, when Patroclus' body lay,
Here Trojan chiefs advanced and there the Greek,*
Ours o'er the Duke their pious wings display
And theirs the noblest spoils of Britain seek.

12

Meantime his busy mariners he hastes
His shattered sails with rigging to restore;
And willing pines ascend his broken masts,
Whose lofty heads rise higher than before.

13

Straight to the Dutch he turns his dreadful prow,
More fierce the important quarrel to decide:
Like swans in long array his vessels show,
Whose crests advancing do the waves divide.

14

They charge, recharge, and all along the sea
They drive and squander the huge Belgian fleet;
Berkeley alone, who nearest danger lay,
Did a like fate with lost Creusa meet.†

15

The night comes on, we eager to pursue
The combat still and they ashamed to leave:
Till the last streaks of dying day withdrew
And doubtful moonlight did our rage deceive.

16

In the English fleet each ship resounds with joy
And loud applause of their great leader's fame;

---

* In the Trojan War, the Greek Patroclus was killed by Hector, who was later slain by Achilles.

† Wife of Aeneas, who lost her husband in the confusion after the fall of Troy and was never reunited with him.

In fiery dreams the Dutch they still destroy,
And slumbering smile at the imagined flame.

17

Not so the Holland fleet, who, tired and done,
Stretched on their decks like weary oxen lie;
Faint sweats all down their mighty members run,
Vast bulks, which little souls but ill supply.

18

In dreams they fearful precipices tread,
Or, shipwracked, labour to some distant shore,
Or in dark churches walk among the dead;
They wake with horror and dare sleep no more.

19

The morn they look on with unwilling eyes,
Till from their maintop joyful news they hear
Of ships which by their mould bring new supplies
And in their colours Belgian lions bear.

20

Our watchful General had discerned from far
This mighty succour, which made glad the foe;
He sighed, but, like a father of the war,
His face spake hope, while deep his sorrows flow.

21

His wounded men he first sends off to shore,
Never till now unwilling to obey:
They not their wounds but want of strength deplore
And think them happy who with him can stay.

22

Then to the rest, "Rejoice," said he, "today
"In you the fortune of Great Britain lies;
"Among so brave a people you are they
"Whom Heaven has chose to fight for such a prize.

23

"If number English courages could quell,
"We should at first have shunned, not met our foes,
"Whose numerous sails the fearful only tell;
"Courage from hearts and not from numbers grows."

24

He said, nor needed more to say: with haste
To their known stations cheerfully they go;
And all at once, disdaining to be last,
Solicit every gale to meet the foe.

25

Nor did the encouraged Belgians long delay,
But bold in others, not themselves, they stood:
So thick, our navy scarce could sheer their way,
But seemed to wander in a moving wood.

26

Our little fleet was now engaged so far
That like the sword-fish in the whale they fought;
The combat only seemed a civil war,
Till through their bowels we our passage wrought.

27

Never had valour, no, not ours before
Done aught like this upon the land or main;
Where not to be o'ercome was to do more
Than all the conquests former Kings did gain.

28

The mighty ghosts of our great Harrys rose,
And armed Edwards looked with anxious eyes,
To see this fleet among unequal foes,
By which fate promised them their Charles should rise.

29

Meantime the Belgians tack upon our rear,
And raking chase-guns* through our sterns they send;

---

* Guns placed at the chase-ports, situated at bows or stern.

Close by, their fire-ships like jackals appear
Who on their lions for the prey attend.

30

Silent in smoke of cannon they come on:
Such vapours once did fiery Cacus hide:*
In these the height of pleased revenge is shown
Who burn contented by another's side.

31

Sometimes from fighting squadrons of each fleet,
Deceived themselves, or to preserve some friend,
Two grappling Aetnas on the ocean meet,
And English fires with Belgian flames contend.

32

Now at each tack our little fleet grows less;
And, like maimed fowl, swim lagging on the main;
Their greater loss their numbers scarce confess,
While they lose cheaper than the English gain.

33

Have you not seen when, whistled from the fist,
Some falcon stoops† at what her eye designed,
And with her eagerness the quarry missed,
Straight flies at check‡ and clips it down the wind;§

34

The dastard crow that to the wood made wing
And sees the groves no shelter can afford,
With her loud caws her craven kind does bring,
Who, safe in numbers, cuff the noble bird.||

---

* A three-headed monster, son of Vulcan, who could emit flames and smoke,
and tried in this way to hide himself from Hercules, who eventually killed him.
† descends, swoops.
‡ being distracted from intended prey.
§ flies rapidly.
|| strike the falcon with their wings.

35

Among the Dutch thus Albermarle did fare:
He could not conquer and disdained to fly:
Past hope of safety, 'twas his latest care,
Like falling Caesar, decently to die.

36

Yet pity did his manly spirit move,
To see those perish who so well had fought;
And generously with his despair he strove,
Resolved to live till he their safety wrought.

37

Let other Muses write his prosperous fate,
Of conquered nations tell and kings restored:
But mine shall sing of his eclipsed estate,
Which, like the sun's, more wonders does afford.

38

He drew his mighty frigates all before,
On which the foe his fruitless force employs;
His weak ones deep into his rear he bore
Remote from guns, as sick men from the noise.

39

His fiery cannon did their passage guide,
And following smoke obscured them from the foe;
Thus Israel, safe from the Egyptian's pride,
By flaming pillars and by clouds did go.*

40

Elsewhere the Belgian force we did defeat,
But here our courages did theirs subdue;
So Xenophon once led that famed retreat†
Which first the Asian empire overthrew.

---

* When the Israelites went out from Egypt, God guided them with a pillar of a cloud by day and a pillar of fire by night. (See Exodus, xiii, 21.)

† Greek general, who led a difficult and prolonged retreat after the battle of Cunaxa against the Persians in 401 B.C.

41

The foe approached; and one for his bold sin
Was sunk, as he that touched the Ark was slain:*
The wild waves mastered him and sucked him in,
And smiling eddies dimpled on the main.

42

This seen, the rest at awful distance stood:
As if they had been there as servants set
To stay or to go on, as he thought good,
And not pursue but wait on his retreat.

43

So Libyan huntsmen on some sandy plain,
From shady coverts roused, the lion chase:
The kingly beast roars out with loud disdain,
And slowly moves, unknowing to give place.

44

But if some one approach to dare his force,
He swings his tail and swiftly turns him round,
With one paw seizes on the trembling horse,
And with the other tears him to the ground.

45

Amidst these toils succeeds the balmy night;
Now hissing waters the quenched guns restore:
And weary waves, withdrawing from the fight,
Lie lulled and panting on the silent shore.

46

The moon shone clear on the becalmed flood,
Where, while her beams like glittering silver play,
Upon the deck our careful General stood,
And deeply mused on the succeeding day.

---

* When the Ark of the Covenant, sacred to the Israelites, was being conveyed
to Jerusalem in the reign of David, Uzza touched it in order to steady it when
the oxen drawing the cart stumbled, and was struck dead for his impiety.
(See 1 Chronicles xiii.)

47

"That happy sun," said he, "will rise again
"Who twice victorious did our navy see,*
"And I alone must view him rise in vain,
"Without one ray of all his star for me.

48

"Yet like an English general will I die,
"And all the ocean make my spacious grave:
"Women and cowards on the land may lie;
"The sea's a tomb that's proper for the brave."

Two of Dryden's own remarks on his poem are of interest here.
First, he considered it an epic poem because of its heroic subject-
matter, although for technical reasons he felt obliged to refer to
it as "historical". Second, he thought it appropriate to describe a
"naval fight in the proper terms which are used at sea". The
first of these comments suggests a comparison with Milton's
Paradise Lost, published in the same year as *Annus Mirabilis* (1667),
since both writers considered they were dealing with subjects
which were worthy of heroic treatment; the second suggests a
contrast, for Dryden was concerned to make the English language
a precise instrument of expression: his membership of the Royal
Society required him to practise in prose "a close, naked, natural
way of speaking; positive expressions; clear senses; a native
easiness", but he brought similar qualities to much of his verse.

Annus Mirabilis is generally regarded as an uneven poem: the
action is sometimes clogged by the required epic impedimenta of
classical and biblical allusions, and Dr. Johnson pointed out that
"he affords more sentiment than description"; but he also con-
sidered verses 15–18 "one of the fairest flowers of English poetry".
Certainly in its more striking passages it possesses a pleasing com-
bination of vigour, directness and elegance in which one is

---

* Naval victories over the Dutch had been won twice before on 3 June, in
1653 and 1665. Albermarle's pessimistic forecast was not fulfilled, for Prince
Rupert's fleet joined him on the third day of the battle.

forcefully assured of the heroism of the English and their leaders ("They not their wounds but want of strength deplore"), and of the miserable cowardice of their enemies ("Vast bulks, which little souls but ill supply").

As well as the suggested contrast with *Paradise Lost* in terms of epic treatment, a further comparison might be made with the account given of a twentieth century sea fight in C. Day Lewis's poem, *The Nabara* (p. 99).

SAMUEL JOHNSON (1709–1784)

PATHS OF GLORY
(From *The Vanity of Human Wishes*)

Johnson wrote this poem (an imitation of the Tenth Satire of Juvenal) to expose the worthlessness of men's worldly ambitions in the spheres of wealth, fame, learning, military glory, longevity and beauty; and reaches the conclusion that only in piety and prayer can real happiness be found. The following lines illustrate the "vanity" of military ambition.

THE festal blazes, the triumphal show,
The ravished standard, and the captive foe,
The senate's thanks, the gazette's pompous tale,
With force resistless o'er the brave prevail.
Such bribes the rapid Greek o'er Asia whirled,
For such the steady Romans shook the world;
For such in distant lands the Britons shine,
And stain with blood the Danube or the Rhine;
This power has praise, that virtue scarce can warm,
10 Till fame supplies the universal charm.
Yet Reason frowns on War's unequal game,
Where wasted nations raise a single name,

And mortgaged states their grandsire's wreaths regret,
From age to age in everlasting debt;
Wreaths which at last the dear-bought right convey
To rust on medals, or on stones decay.

On what foundation stands the warrior's pride,
How just his hopes let Swedish Charles decide;
A frame of adamant, a soul of fire,
20 No dangers fright him, and no labours tire;
O'er love, o'er fear, extends his wide domain,
Unconquered lord of pleasure and of pain;
No joys to him pacific sceptres yield,
War sounds the trump, he rushes to the field;
Behold surrounding kings their power combine,
And one capitulate, and one resign;
Peace courts his hand, but spreads her charms in vain;
"Think nothing gained," he cries, "till nought remain,
"On Moscow's walls till Gothic standards fly,
30 "And all be mine beneath the polar sky."
The march begins in military state,
And nations on his eye suspended wait;
Stern Famine guards the solitary coast,
And Winter barricades the realms of Frost;
He comes, not want and cold his course delay;—
Hide, blushing Glory, hide Pultowa's day:
The vanquished hero leaves his broken bands,
And shows his miseries in distant lands;
Condemned a needy supplicant to wait,
40 While ladies interpose, and slaves debate.
But did not Chance at length her error mend?
Did no subverted empire mark his end?
Did rival monarchs give the fatal wound?
Or hostile millions press him to the ground?
His fall was destined to a barren strand,
A petty fortress, and a dubious hand;
He left the name, at which the world grew pale,
To point a moral, or adorn a tale.

All times their scenes of pompous woe afford,
50 From Persia's tyrant to Bavaria's lord.
In gay hostility, and barbarous pride,
With half mankind embattled at his side,
Great Xerxes comes to seize the certain prey,
And starves exhausted regions in his way;
Attendant Flattery counts his millions o'er,
Till counted myriads soothe his pride no more;
Fresh praise is tried till madness fires his mind,
The waves he lashes, and enchains the wind;
New powers are claimed, new powers are still bestowed,
60 Till rude resistance lops the spreading god;
The daring Greeks deride the martial show,
And heap their valleys with the gaudy foe;
The insulted sea with humbler thoughts he gains,
A single skiff to speed his flight remains;
The incumbered oar scarce leaves the dreaded coast
Through purple billows and a floating host.
The bold Bavarian, in a luckless hour,
Tries the dread summits of Caesarian power,
With unexpected legions bursts away,
70 And sees defenceless realms receive his sway;
Short sway! fair Austria spreads her mournful charms,
The queen, the beauty, sets the world in arms;
From hill to hill the beacons' rousing blaze
Spreads wide the hope of plunder and of praise;
The fierce Croatian and the wild Hussar,
And all the sons of ravage crowd the war;
The baffled prince in honour's flattering bloom
Of hasty greatness finds the fatal doom,
His foes' derision, and his subjects' blame,
80 And steals to death from anguish and from shame.

As some initial difficulty may be experienced with this extract
because of the historical allusions, a brief explanation of these may
be useful.

After commenting on the inability of brave men to resist the glories of victory (lines 1–4), Johnson cites the examples of the campaigns of Alexander the Great ("the rapid Greek"), the conquests of the Romans, and battles in which the British had recently taken part (in the 1740's). The "single name" (l. 12) is a reference to the Duke of Marlborough.

The next section of the passage (lines 17–48) is concerned with the career of Charles XII of Sweden, well known in Johnson's day for his remarkably aggressive character and exploits. The "surrounding kings" (l. 25) are those of Denmark, Poland and Russia, and line 36 refers to the defeat of Charles at Pultowa in 1709 by Peter the Great, whose empress, Catherine, later helped to negotiate a settlement whereby Charles was to return to Sweden from exile in Turkey (l. 40). The concluding lines of this section are concerned with Charles's unheroic death by a stray bullet while besieging a minor Norwegian fortress in 1718.

The final sections deal with Xerxes, King of Persia (519–465 B.C.), who invaded Greece and, according to Herodotus, ordered the Hellespont to be lashed and chained when his bridge across it was destroyed in a storm; and the Emperor Charles VII, Elector of Bavaria, who overran Bohemia and Austria (l. 70) until checked by the armies, raised by Maria Theresa (l. 72), which invaded his kingdom.

Although specific knowledge of Johnson's historical examples may help to clarify the surface meaning of the extract, it should be understood that the real significance of the piece lies in the use of particular instances to establish a general truth, and so affirm the poet's belief in the futility of human ambition. This he does by a controlled and assured use of language with the words carefully selected, the rhythms subtly varied, to achieve the maximum effectiveness. T. S. Eliot has described *The Vanity of Human Wishes* as one of the finest verse satires in any language, and the whole poem will repay close study for the peculiar satisfaction that can be found in the best Augustan poetry. This extract is not primarily a denunciation of the military life (Johnson had a high regard for soldiers), but looks upon war, from the vantage point of a stoic philosophy, as one instance of man's pretentiousness and folly.

WILLIAM COWPER (1731–1800)

THE MILITIAMAN

(From *The Task*, Book IV)

Cowper's poem had its origin in the suggestion made to the poet by his friend, Lady Austen (who also gave him his subject-matter for *John Gilpin*), that he should compose a poem in blank verse on the subject of his sofa. This, his "task", began in a light-hearted, mock-epic manner, but went on discursively and in a variety of moods as topics for description and reflection came to his mind. In the following lines, having just deplored the declining standards of country life, he comments on the disastrous effects upon the simple countryman of three years in the militia.

> But faster far, and more than all the rest,
> A noble cause, which none who bears a spark
> Of public virtue ever wished removed,
> Works the deplored and mischievous effect.
> 'Tis universal soldiership has stabbed
> The heart of merit in the meaner class.
> Arms, through the vanity and brainless rage
> Of those that bear them, in whatever cause,
> Seem most at variance with all moral good,
> 10 And incompatible with serious thought.
> The clown, the child of nature, without guile,
> Blest with an infant's ignorance of all
> But his own simple pleasures; now and then
> A wrestling-match, a foot-race, or a fair;

Is ballotted, and trembles at the news:
Sheepish he doffs his hat, and, mumbling, swears
A bible-oath to be whate'er they please,
To do he knows not what! The task performed,
That instant he becomes the serjeant's care,
20 His pupil, and his torment, and his jest.
His awkward gait, his introverted toes,
Bent knees, round shoulders, and dejected looks,
Procure him many a curse. By slow degrees,
Unapt to learn, and formed of stubborn stuff,
He yet by slow degrees puts off himself,
Grows conscious of a change, and likes it well:
He stands erect; his slouch becomes a walk;
He steps right onward, martial in his air,
His form and movement; is as smart above
30 As meal and larded locks can make him; wears
His hat, or his plumed helmet, with a grace;
And, his three years of heroship expired,
Returns indignant to the slighted plough.
He hates the field, in which no fife or drum
Attends him; drives his cattle to a march;
And sighs for the smart comrades he has left.
'Twere well if his exterior change were all—
But with his clumsy port the wretch has lost
His ignorance and harmless manners too!
40 To swear, to game, to drink; to show at home
By lewdness, idleness, and sabbath-breach,
The great proficiency he made abroad;
To astonish and to grieve his gazing friends,
To break some maiden's and his mother's heart;
To be a pest where he was useful once;
Are his sole aim, and all his glory, now!
   Man in society is like a flower
Blown in its native bed: 'tis there alone
His faculties, expanded in full bloom,
50 Shine out; there only reach their proper use.

But man, associated and leagued with man
By regal warrant, or self-joined by bond
For interest-sake, or swarming into clans
Beneath one head for purposes of war,
Like flowers selected from the rest, and bound
And bundled close to fill some crowded vase,
Fades rapidly, and, by compression marred,
Contracts defilement not to be endured.
Hence chartered boroughs are such public plagues;
60   And burghers, men immaculate perhaps
In all their private functions, once combined,
Become a loathsome body, only fit
For dissolution, hurtful to the main.
Hence merchants, unimpeachable of sin
Against the charities of domestic life,
Incorporated, seem at once to lose
Their nature; and disclaiming all regard
For mercy and the common rights of man,
Build factories with blood, conducting trade
70   At the sword's point, and dyeing the white robe
Of innocent commercial justice red.
Hence, too, the field of glory, as the world
Misdeems it, dazzled by its bright array,
With all its majesty of thundering pomp,
Enchanting music, and immortal wreaths,
Is but a school where thoughtlessness is taught
On principle, where foppery atones
For folly, gallantry for every vice.

Cowper's lines make an interesting contrast with those of
Johnson in the previous passage. Both are, to some extent, de-
nouncing the "vanity" of militarism; but it is characteristic of
Johnson's manner that he should be concerned with general
truths, and of Cowper's that he should dwell upon the individual
victim of the militia system. Cowper certainly does generalize,
both in the opening and at the close of this extract, and there are

some spirited passages of denunciation contained in these lines; but the more appealing section is that which describes the transformation of the innocent bumpkin into the pretentious temporary soldier (lines 11–46), for here there is sympathetic observation of a real person caught up in the ugly machinery of the state. There are some moments in the passage which bring to mind Falstaff's recruits in *Henry IV*, Part 2, and others which have a ring of truth to them distinctly audible to contemporary ears.

The modern reader may feel there is something naïve about Cowper's attitude towards his "child of nature", and in the attitude that is implied concerning the social order; but there is nevertheless a strength and seriousness in his verse which arises from a compassionate concern for human beings and an indignation at the corruption of values which he cherishes. In these lines we can hear the quiet but firm voice of an unassuming man who is moved to protest against what he considers a social evil; and the voice commands respect because it is both honest and humane.

THOMAS CAMPBELL (1777–1844)

HOHENLINDEN

The battle of Hohenlinden took place in a forest near Munich at the beginning of December, 1800, when the French Revolutionary army inflicted a decisive defeat on the Austrians. Campbell, who was touring Germany at this time, may have witnessed the battle, and certainly visited the battlefield.

> ON LINDEN, when the sun was low,
> All bloodless lay the untrodden snow;
> And dark as winter was the flow
> Of Iser, rolling rapidly.

But Linden saw another sight,
When the drum beat at dead of night,
Commanding fires of death to light
   The darkness of her scenery.

By torch and trumpet fast arrayed
Each horseman drew his battle blade
And furious every charger neighed
   To join the dreadful revelry.

Then shook the hills with thunder riven,
Then rushed the steed, to battle driven,
And louder than the bolts of Heaven
   Far flashed the red artillery.

But redder yet that light shall glow
On Linden's hills of stainéd snow;
And bloodier yet the torrent flow
   Of Iser, rolling rapidly.

'Tis morn; but scarce yon level sun
Can pierce the war-clouds, rolling dun,
Where furious Frank and fiery Hun
   Shout in their sulphurous canopy.

The combat deepens. On, ye brave
Who rush to glory, or the grave!
Wave, Munich, all thy banners wave,
   And charge with all thy chivalry!

Few, few shall part, where many meet!
The snow shall be their winding-sheet,
And every turf beneath their feet
   Shall be a soldier's sepulchre.

Hohenlinden enjoyed considerable popularity for many years as a stirring battle poem, and, together with the same author's *Battle of the Baltic* and *Lord Ullin's Daughter*, was a favourite in the classroom—with teachers, if not their pupils. Although today's more sophisticated tastes may prefer to consign it to the decent seclusion of *The Golden Treasury* (where Campbell is quite lavishly represented), the fact that it represents a distinct type of war poetry, and is a good example of that type, may justify its inclusion here.

The merit of the poem lies in its craftsmanship. Through his choice of stanza-form and metre, his rhyme-scheme, alliterative and onomatopoeic effects, Campbell creates, with skilful economy, an atmosphere of menace, felt in the urgent beat of the rhythm, and a sense of excitement as the drama of the battle is unfolded in colourful imagery.

But this very sense of the dramatic suggests why, to the modern reader, the poem is not entirely acceptable, for we feel that the pageantry of the occasion is being exploited at the expense of reality. The scarlet blood-stains contrasting vividly with the pure white of the snow, the firelight and artillery flashes set against the darkness of the night, the call to death or glory, and the properly solemn elegiacs of the concluding stanza are all elements in a splendid spectacle rather than an account of warfare and carnage in which actual human beings are involved.

Campbell exercises his technical skill effectively and produces some fine imaginative flourishes, but the final impression is unsatisfying because it is difficult today to think of a battle as a means of providing edifying entertainment for the casual onlooker.

LORD BYRON (1788–1824)

THE EVE OF WATERLOO

(From *Childe Harold's Pilgrimage*, Canto 3)

Childe Harold's Pilgrimage tells of the wanderings through Europe of its disillusioned hero and of his reflections on the places he visits. In Canto 3 he passes through Belgium, Germany and

Switzerland, and the following famous lines describe the ball held in Brussels on the night before the battle, and its disruption at the news of Napoleon's impending attack.

1

THERE was a sound of revelry by night,
And Belgium's capital had gathered then
Her Beauty and her Chivalry, and bright
The lamps shone o'er fair women and brave men;
A thousand hearts beat happily; and when
Music arose with its voluptuous swell,
Soft eyes looked love to eyes which spake again,
And all went merry as a marriage-bell;
But hush! hark! a deep sound strikes like a rising knell!

2

Did ye not hear it?—No; 'twas but the wind
Or the car rattling o'er the stony street;
On with the dance! let joy be unconfined;
No sleep till morn, when Youth and Pleasure meet
To chase the glowing Hours with flying feet—
But, hark!—that heavy sound breaks in once more
As if the clouds its echo would repeat;
And nearer, clearer, deadlier than before!
Arm! Arm! it is—it is—the cannon's opening roar!

3

Within a windowed niche of that high hall
Sate Brunswick's fated chieftain; he did hear
That sound the first amidst the festival,
And caught its tone with Death's prophetic ear;
And when they smiled because he deemed it near,
His heart more truly knew that peal too well
Which stretched his father on a bloody bier,*

---

* The Duke of Brunswick's father was killed at Jena.

And roused the vengeance blood alone could quell:
He rushed into the field, and, foremost fighting, fell.

4

Ah! then and there was hurrying to and fro,
And gathering tears, and tremblings of distress,
And cheeks all pale, which but an hour ago
Blushed at the praise of their own loveliness;
And there were sudden partings, such as press
The life from out young hearts, and choking sighs
Which ne'er might be repeated; who could guess
If ever more should meet those mutual eyes,
Since upon night so sweet such awful morn could rise!

5

And there was mounting in hot haste: the steed,
The mustering squadron, and the clattering car,
Went pouring forward with impetuous speed,
And swiftly forming in the ranks of war;
And the deep thunder peal on peal afar;
And near, the beat of the alarming drum
Roused up the soldier ere the morning star;
While thronged the citizens with terror dumb,
Or whispering, with white lips—"The foe! they come! they
    come!"

6

And wild and high the "Cameron's gathering" rose!
The war-note of Lochiel, which Albyn's hills
Have heard, and heard, too, have her Saxon foes:—
How in the noon of night that pibroch thrills,
Savage and shrill! But with the breath which fills
Their mountain-pipe, so fill the mountaineers
With the fierce native daring which instils
The stirring memory of a thousand years,
And Evan's, Donald's fame rings in each clansman's ears!

7

And Ardennes waves above them her green leaves,
Dewy with nature's tear-drops, as they pass,
Grieving, if aught inanimate e'er grieves,
Over the unreturning brave,—alas!
Ere evening to be trodden like the grass
Which now beneath them, but above shall grow
In its next verdure, when this fiery mass
Of living valour, rolling on the foe
And burning with high hope shall moulder cold and low.

8

Last noon beheld them full of lusty life,
Last eve in Beauty's circle proudly gay,
The midnight brought the signal-sound of strife,
The morn the marshalling in arms,—the day
Battle's magnificently stern array!
The thunder-clouds close o'er it, which when rent
The earth is covered thick with other clay,
Which her own clay shall cover, heaped and pent,
Rider and horse,—friend, foe,—in one red burial blent!

"THE TRUE PORTRAIT . . ."

(From *Don Juan*, Canto 8)

Byron's *Don Juan* tells the remarkable story of its attractive and
amorous hero in a variety of adventures in Spain, Greece, Turkey,
Russia and England. In Cantos 7 and 8, Don Juan, having
sought refuge in the Russian army, becomes involved in the siege
of Ismail. The following stanzas give some indication of Byron's
treatment of war in this poem.

1

Oh BLOOD and thunder! and oh blood and wounds!
   These are but vulgar oaths, as you may deem,
Too gentle reader! and most shocking sounds:
   And so they are; yet thus is Glory's dream
Unriddled, and as my true Muse expounds
   At present such things, since they are her theme,
So be they her inspirers! Call them Mars,
Bellona, what you will—they mean but wars.

2

All was prepared—the fire, the sword, the men
   To wield them in their terrible array:
The army, like a lion from his den,
   Marched forth with nerve and sinews bent to slay,—
A human Hydra, issuing from its fen
   To breathe destruction on its winding way,
Whose heads were heroes, which cut off in vain,
Immediately in others grew again.

3

History can only take things in the gross;
   But could we know them in detail, perchance
In balancing the profit and the loss,
   War's merit it by no means might enhance,
To waste so much gold for a little dross,
   As hath been done, mere conquest to advance.
The drying up a single tear has more
Of honest fame, than shedding seas of gore.

4

And why?—because it brings self-approbation;
   Whereas the other, after all its glare,
Shouts, bridges, arches, pensions, from a nation,
   Which (it may be) has not much left to spare,

A higher title, or a loftier station
    Though they may make Corruption gape or stare,
Yet, in the end, except in Freedom's battles,
Are nothing but a child of Murder's rattles.

5

And such they are—and such they will be found:
    Not so Leonidas* and Washington,
Whose every battlefield is holy ground,
    Which breathes of nations saved, not worlds undone.
How sweetly on the ear such echoes sound!
    While the mere victors may appal or stun
The servile and the vain, such names will be
A watchword till the future shall be free.

6

The night was dark, and the thick mist allowed
    Nought to be seen but the artillery's flame,
Which arched the horizon like a fiery cloud,
    And in the Danube's waters shone the same—
A mirrored hell! the volleying roar, and loud
    Long booming of each peal on peal, o'ercame
The ear far more than thunder; for Heaven's flashes
Spare, or smite rarely—man's make million ashes!

7

Three hundred cannon threw up their emetic,
    And thirty thousand muskets flung their pills
Like hail, to make a bloody diuretic.
    Mortality! thou hast thy monthly bills;
Thy plagues, thy famines, thy physicians, yet tick,
    Like the death-watch, within our ears the ills,

---

* King of Sparta, and hero of the defence of Thermopylae against the army
of Xerxes.

Past, present, and to come;—but all may yield
To the true portrait of one battle-field.

8

There the still varying pangs, which multiply
    Until their very number makes men hard
By the infinities of agony,
    Which meet the gaze, whate'er it may regard—
The groan, the roll in dust, the all-white eye
    Turned back within its socket,—these reward
Your rank and file by thousands, while the rest
May win perhaps a riband at the breast!

9

Yet I love glory;—glory's a great thing:—
    Think what it is to be in your old age
Maintained at the expense of your good king:
    A moderate pension shakes full many a sage,
And heroes are but made for bards to sing,
    Which is still better; thus in verse to wage
Your wars eternally, besides enjoying
Half-pay for life, make mankind worth destroying.

These two extracts represent completely contrasting aspects of
Byron's poetry. Both *Childe Harold's Pilgrimage* and *Don Juan* have
itinerant heroes, but Childe Harold is morose and romantic while
Don Juan is a carefree sensualist, and these contrasting central
characters are set in verse contexts appropriate to their respective
roles, as can be seen from the brief extracts quoted here.

Childe Harold was an immediate popular success, its dramatic
rhetoric winning acclaim not only in England but in France and
Germany. The lines on the eve of Waterloo have been described
by one contemporary critic as "claptrap", and we have to acknow-
ledge the presence of some of the cruder elements in romanticism:
posturing and bombast, with descents into the kind of senti-

mentality found in the first four lines of stanza 7 (compare Wilfred Owen's treatment of this idea in the third stanza of *Spring Offensive*); but there is a wholeheartedness about the fustian language and a vigour in the exclamatory style that carries the reader along in spite of any fastidious reluctance he may feel to be moved—even by the poignancy of the parting lovers and the ominous prophesying of death.

In *Don Juan* Byron abandoned pretentiousness and straining after effect, and produced in this vast mock-epic satire a style of verse—colloquial, mocking, tremendously exuberant—which was exactly suited to his particular genius. It is impossible to give a satisfactory sample of the poem within the limitations of the present anthology, for *Don Juan* must be read at length for its full effects to be appreciated, but even in this short extract can be sensed the powerful zest of the writing, the fluent conversational tone, the capacity for biting contempt, and a kind of savage sincerity in his attitude to war which looks forward to the angry bitterness of Sassoon and Owen.

The sheer energy of Byron's satirical manner may seem very far removed from the solemn voice of Dr. Johnson, but both in their characteristic ways were using the instrument of satire for the same purpose (as Mr. J. D. Jump* has pointed out); for the criticism of life made explicit in *The Vanity of Human Wishes* is in essence the same as that which, despite much superficial flippancy and a very different approach, is implicit in *Don Juan*. Johnson's moral purpose is clearly defined; Byron indicates his attitude when he says, in Canto 12:

> I mean to show things really as they are,
> Not as they ought to be: for I avow,
>   That till we see what's what in fact, we're far
> From much improvement.

---

* In his essay on Byron in *The Pelican Guide to English Literature*, Volume 5.

Lord Tennyson (1809–1892)

THE DEFENCE OF LUCKNOW

The siege of Lucknow was one of the most famous episodes of the Indian Mutiny of 1857. It began on 1 July when the garrison of about 1700 men under the command of Sir Henry Lawrence (who was killed at the opening of the siege) defended the residency and its community of over 1000 non-combatants against incessant attack from close range by 6000 trained rebel soldiers and a very large number of irregulars. Relief eventually came on 25 September, when a force under the command of General Havelock and Sir James Outram entered the city.

1

Banner of England, not for a season, O banner of Britain, hast thou
Floated in conquering battle or flapt to the battle cry!
Never with mightier glory than when we had reared thee on high
Flying at top of the roofs in the ghastly siege of Lucknow—
Shot thro' the staff or the halyard, but ever we raised thee anew,
And ever upon the topmost roof our banner of England blew.

2

Frail were the works that defended the hold that we held with our lives—
Women and children among us, God help them, our children and wives!
Hold it we might—and for fifteen days or for twenty at most.
"Never surrender, I charge you, but every man die at his post!"

Voice of the dead whom we loved, our Lawrence the best of
 the brave:
Cold were his brows when we kissed him—we laid him that
 night in his grave.
"Every man die at his post!" and there hailed on our houses
 and halls
Death from their rifle-bullets, and death from their
 cannon-balls,
Death in our innermost chamber, and death at our slight
 barricade,
Death while we stood with the musket, and death while we
 stoopt to the spade,
Death to the dying, and wounds to the wounded, for often
 there fell,
Striking the hospital wall, crashing thro' it, their shot and
 their shell,
Death—for their spies were among us, their marksmen were
 told of our best,
So that the brute bullet broke thro' the brain that could
 think for the rest;
Bullets would sing by our foreheads, and bullets would rain
 at our feet—
Fire from ten thousand at once of the rebels that girdled us
 round—
Death at the glimpse of a finger from over the breadth of a
 street,
Death from the heights of the mosque and the palace, and
 death in the ground!
Mine? Yes, a mine! Countermine! down, down! and creep
 thro' the hole!
Keep the revolver in hand! you can hear him—the murderous
 mole!
Quiet, ah! quiet—wait till the point of the pickaxe be
 thro'!
Click with the pick, coming nearer and nearer again than
 before—

Now let it speak, and you fire, and the dark pioneer is no
    more;
And ever upon the topmost roof our banner of England blew!

3

Ay, but the foe sprung his mine many times, and it chanced
    on a day
Soon as the blast of that underground thunderclap echoed
    away,
Dark thro' the smoke and the sulphur like so many fiends in
    their hell—
Cannon-shot, musket-shot, volley on volley, and yell upon yell—
Fiercely on all the defences our myriad enemy fell.
What have they done? where is it? Out yonder. Guard the
    Redan!
Storm at the Water-gate! storm at the Bailey-gate! storm, and
    it ran
Surging and swaying all round us, as ocean on every side
Plunges and heaves at a bank that is daily drowned by the tide—
So many thousands that if they be bold enough, who shall
    escape?
Kill or be killed, live or die, they shall know we are soldiers
    and men!
Ready! take aim at their leaders—their masses are gapped
    with our grape—
Backward they reel like the wave, like the wave flinging
    forward again,
Flying and foiled at the last by the handful they could not
    subdue;
And ever upon the topmost roof our banner of England blew.

4

Handful of men as we were, we were English in heart and in
    limb,
Strong with the strength of the race to command, to obey, to
    endure,

Each of us fought as if hope for the garrison hung but on him;
Still—could we watch at all points? we were every day fewer
 and fewer.
There was a whisper among us, but only a whisper that
 past:
"Children and wives—if the tigers leap into the fold
 unawares—
Every man die at his post—and the foe may outlive us at
 last—
Better to fall by the hands that they love, than to fall into
 theirs!"
Roar upon roar in a moment two mines by the enemy sprung
Clove into perilous chasms our walls and our poor palisades.
Rifleman, true is your heart, but be sure that your hand be
 as true!
Sharp is the fire of assault, better aimed are your flank
 fusilades—
Twice do we hurl them to earth from the ladders to which
 they had clung,
Twice from the ditch where they shelter we drive them with
 hand-grenades;
And ever upon the topmost roof our banner of England blew.

5

Then on another wild morning another wild earthquake
 out-tore
Clean from our lines of defence ten or twelve good paces or
 more.
Riflemen high on the roof, hidden there from the light of the
 sun—
One has leapt up on the breach, crying out: "Follow me,
 follow me!"—
Mark him—he falls! then another, and *him* too, and down
 goes he.
Had they been bold enough then, who can tell but the
 traitors had won?

Boardings and rafters and doors—an embrasure! make way
    for the gun!
Now double-charge it with grape! It is charged and we fire,
    and they run.
Praise to our Indian brothers, and let the dark face have his
    due!
Thanks to the kindly dark faces who fought with us, faithful
    and few,
Fought with the bravest among us, and drove them, and
    smote them, and slew,
That ever upon the topmost roof our banner in India blew.

6

Men will forget what we suffer and not what we do. We can
    fight
But to be soldier all day and be sentinel all thro' the night—
Ever the mine and assault, our sallies, their lying alarms.
Bugles and drums in the darkness, and shoutings and soundings
    to arms,
Ever the labour of fifty that had to be done by five,
Ever the marvel among us that one should be left alive,
Ever the day with its traitorous death from the loopholes
    around,
Ever the night with its coffinless corpse to be laid in the
    ground,
Heat like the mouth of a hell, or a deluge of cataract skies,
Stench of old offal decaying, and infinite torment of flies,
Thoughts of the breezes of May blowing over an English
    field,
Cholera, scurvy, and fever, the wound that *would* not be
    healed,
Lopping away of the limb by the pitiful-pitiless knife,—
Torture and trouble in vain,—for it never could save us a life.
Valour of delicate women who tended the hospital bed,
Horror of women in travail among the dying and dead,
Grief for our perishing children, and never a moment for grief,

Toil and ineffable weariness, faltering hopes of relief,
Havelock baffled, or beaten, or butchered for all that we
    knew—
Then day and night, day and night, coming down on the
    still-shattered walls
Millions of musket-bullets, and thousands of cannon-balls—
But ever upon the topmost roof our banner of England blew.

7

Hark cannonade, fusillade! is it true what was told by the
    scout,
Outram and Havelock breaking their way through the fell
    mutineers?
Surely the pibroch of Europe is ringing again in our ears!
All on a sudden the garrison utter a jubilant shout,
Havelock's glorious Highlanders answer with conquering
    cheers,
Sick from the hospital echo them, women and children come
    out,
Blessing the wholesome white faces of Havelock's good
    fusiliers,
Kissing the war-hardened hand of the Highlander wet with
    their tears!
Dance to the pibroch!—saved! we are saved!—is it you? is it
    you?
Saved by the valour of Havelock, saved by the blessing of
    Heaven!
"Hold it for fifteen days!" we have held it for eighty-seven!
And ever aloft on the palace roof the old banner of England
    blew.

This piece represents the type of war poetry that attempts to
recreate a real and contemporary battle situation. Dryden did
this in *Annus Mirabilis* and Campbell in *Hohenlinden*, but whereas
Dryden's narrative is cast in a lofty, epic style and Campbell's in
the manner of the detached spectator, Tennyson has tried to

re-live the action (some years after the event) by putting himself behind the barricades at Lucknow and becoming the poet as reporter.

Sir Alfred Lyall, writing within a decade of the death of Tennyson, examined this poem and found that in spite of its "abundance of fiery animation" there was "too much vehemence and tumultuous activity;. . . . he accumulates authentic details, he tries to give us the scenes and events with the roar of battle, the terror and the misery;" but "one must pass upon it the criticism that the canvas is overcrowded and the verse too hurried and vehement . . .". Tennyson is certainly trying to convey the hectic confusion of the battle scene and to some readers his use of laboured hexameters and an exclamatory manner may seem to create confusion in the verse. But, in spite of a certain unwieldiness, the poem has a fierce, defiant tone which manages to overcome the cumbrous verse-form. Tennyson took very seriously his role as Poet Laureate, and the sincerity of his Victorian patriotism emerges strongly from these lines in which the horror of the situation and the desperate courage of those involved in it are conveyed with a kind of dogged fervour. Although the heroics of imperialism get little sympathy in contemporary taste, *The Defence of Lucknow* still elicits a response because it celebrates the qualities of courage and endurance which are admirable, whatever their historical context.

THOMAS HARDY (1840–1928)

THE ROAD TO WATERLOO

(From *The Dynasts*, Part 3, Act VI, Scene VIII)

The Dynasts is an epic-drama of the Napoleonic Wars, written mainly in blank verse, recounting the historical events and the parts played by the principals involved, but also including episodes showing how the war touched the lives of ordinary people. There are comments, too, from Spirits—"supernatural spectators of the terrestial action"—who are introduced to give a universal significance to the narrative as it unfolds. The following lines come from a passage in which three of the Choruses of Spirits presage the battle of Waterloo. The scene is set in Hardy's own words.

Fires begin to shine up from the English bivouacs. Camp kettles are slung, and the men pile arms and stand round the blaze to dry themselves. The French opposite lie down like dead men in the dripping green wheat and rye, without supper and without fire.

By and by the English army also lies down, the men huddling together on the ploughed mud in their wet blankets, while some sleep sitting round the dying fires.

Chorus of the Years (Aerial music)

The eyelids of eve fall together at last,
And the forms so foreign to field and tree
Lie down as though native, and slumber fast!

Chorus of the Pities

Sore are the thrills of misgiving we see
In the artless champaign of this harlequinade,
Distracting a vigil where calm should be!

The green seems opprest, and the Plain afraid
Of a Something to come, whereof these are the proofs,—
Neither earthquake, nor storm, nor eclipse's shade!

Chorus of the Years

Yea, the coneys are scared by the thud of hoofs,
And their white scuts flash at their vanishing heels,
And swallows abandon the hamlet-roofs.

The mole's tunnelled chambers are crushed by wheels,
The lark's eggs scattered, their owners fled;
And the hedgehog's household the sapper unseals.

The snail draws in at the terrible tread,
But in vain; he is crushed by the felloe-rim;
The worm asks what can be overhead,

And wriggles deep from a scene so grim,
And guesses him safe; for he does not know
What a foul red flood will be soaking him!

Beaten about by the heel and toe
Are butterflies, sick of the day's long rheum,
To die of a worse than the weather-foe.

Trodden and bruised to a miry tomb
Are ears that have greened but will never be gold,
And flowers in the bud that will never bloom.

Chorus of the Pities

So the season's intent, ere its fruit unfold,
Is frustrate, and mangled, and made succumb,
Like a youth of promise struck stark and cold! . . .

And what of these who tonight have come?

Chorus of the Years

The young sleep sound; but the weather awakes
In the veterans, pains from the past that numb;

Old stabs of Ind, old Peninsular aches,
Old Friedland chills, haunt their moist mud bed,
Cramps from Austerlitz; till their slumber breaks.

Chorus of Sinister Spirits

And each soul shivers as sinks his head
On the loam he's to lease with the other dead
From tomorrow's mist-fall till Time be sped!

The fires of the English go out, and silence prevails, save for the soft hiss of the rain that falls impartially on both the sleeping armies.

IN TIME OF "THE BREAKING OF NATIONS"*
(1915)

I

ONLY a man harrowing clods
  In a slow silent walk
With an old horse that stumbles and nods
  Half asleep as they stalk.

II

Only thin smoke without flame
  From the heaps of couch-grass:
Yet this will go onward the same
  Though Dynasties pass.

III

Yonder a maid and her wight
  Come whispering by:
War's annals will fade into night
  Ere their story die.

CHRISTMAS, 1924

"PEACE upon earth!" was said. We sing it,
And pay a million priests to bring it.
After two thousand years of mass
We've got as far as poison-gas.

These three passages span about 100 years of warfare, from the
immediate forebodings of an actual battlefield in 1815 to the

* "Thou art my battle axe and weapons of war: for with thee will I break in
pieces the nations, and with thee will I destroy kingdoms." Jeremiah, 51, 20.

implied and pessimistic prediction of 1924. Each is illuminated by Hardy's sense of perspective. Within his vast panorama of the Napoleonic Wars he sees the English and French soldiers against a background of Time and the seasons, the natural world shattered and terrified by the ruthlessness of man, but the men themselves little more than sad puppets on the world's stage. The quiet and assured tone of the second piece shows this sense of perspective even more clearly, for here war is seen as a mere background to the basic and enduring things in human life that will survive the disasters of history. The terse, epigrammatic poem on *Christmas, 1924* presents a bitter and cynical view of man's spiritual progress over the centuries, and shows Hardy's capacity for a cruel pessimism—not entirely belied by subsequent events.

While the last poem is not quite characteristic of Hardy's most successful manner, the other two passages, with their idiosyncrasies of vocabulary and expression, represent him at his best, for they are imbued with the poet's own brooding melancholy, which so often appeared in the novels, with their disturbingly tragic view of life. The compassion of the passage from *The Dynasts* and the tranquil strength of *In Time of "The Breaking of Nations"* show us a view of war firmly stamped with Hardy's own personality.

W. B. YEATS (1865–1939)

ON BEING ASKED FOR A WAR POEM

I THINK it better that in times like these
A poet's mouth be silent, for in truth
We have no gift to set a statesman right;
He has had enough of meddling who can please
A young girl in the indolence of her youth,
Or an old man upon a winter's night.

AN IRISH AIRMAN FORESEES HIS DEATH

I KNOW that I shall meet my fate
Somewhere among the clouds above;
Those that I fight I do not hate,
Those that I guard I do not love;
My country is Kiltartan Cross,
My countrymen Kiltartan's poor,
No likely end could bring them loss
Or leave them happier than before.
Nor law, nor duty bade me fight,
Nor public men, nor cheering crowds,
A lonely impulse of delight
Drove to this tumult in the clouds;
I balanced all, brought all to mind,
The years to come seemed waste of breath,
A waste of breath the years behind
In balance with this life, this death.

Like Thomas Hardy, Yeats was no longer young when war broke out in 1914, and so both were capable of the kind of detachment in writing about the war that might have been impossible in younger men. But in Yeats there is an additional aloofness which comes partly from temperament and partly from the Irish nationalism which dominated much of his life and work.

In his refusal to write "a war poem" there is a contemptuous impatience at the suggestion that he should seek "to set a statesman right" and a contentment in doing the job of a poet, not that of a political propagandist: an attitude expressed with an economy of means and an authority of tone which silence criticism.

The same economy and authority are present in his lines on the Irish airman, where he is in fact writing his most famous "war poem", but, characteristically, preserves the aloofness and sees the role of the airman not as that of a combatant patriotically fighting an enemy, but of a man responding to the challenge of the "tumult in the clouds" and seeking a mystical fulfilment in the knowledge of danger and the certainty of death. This is a poem about war not as a clash between rival nations or as the source of the suffering of the people engaged in it, but as a means for an individual to find his own personal consummation in its impersonal violence and destruction.

RUPERT BROOKE (1887–1915)

THE SOLDIER

IF I should die, think only this of me:
    That there's some corner of a foreign field
That is for ever England. There shall be
    In that rich earth a richer dust concealed;
A dust whom England bore, shaped, made aware,
    Gave, once, her flowers to love, her ways to roam,
A body of England's, breathing English air,
    Washed by the rivers, blest by suns of home.

And think, this heart, all evil shed away,
    A pulse in the eternal mind, no less,
        Gives somewhere back the thoughts by England given;
Her sights and sounds; dreams happy as her day;
    And laughter, learnt of friends; and gentleness,
        In hearts at peace, under an English heaven.

There is a sad irony surrounding the once almost legendary figure of Rupert Brooke that is enhanced by the fame that has accrued to this poem. The irony lies in the innocence and naïvety of *The Soldier* as a "war poem", for Brooke, although eagerly enlisting in 1914 and prepared to die for his country, in fact saw little action and died of blood-poisoning while on his way to Gallipoli.

Brooke, with his romantic good-looks, attractive personality, his literary reputation and considerable ability, was made into a kind of young Apollo by his contemporaries, and his death as a soldier came to symbolize the loss of a generation of young men. In fact he was typical neither as soldier nor poet, for he did not live to experience the horrors of Flanders, and as a result he was not able to write about the war as men like Sassoon and Owen came to write about it. His sonnet is a skilfully composed tribute to an England which had blessed him more liberally than it had many who were to die for her, and is a sincere expression of his devotion; but the skill and sincerity of the poem have the effect of toning down the somewhat arrogant patriotism implied in the "richer dust" allusion, although one feels that the arrogance was unconscious and the patriotism genuine. Its experience, however, is of an utterly different world from that of Sassoon's *Memorial Tablet* (p. 85) or Owen's "happy" soldier in *Insensibility* (p. 90): a contrast which is unfair to Brooke, but which, in the context of war poetry, will inevitably be made.

LAURENCE BINYON (1869–1943)

FOR THE FALLEN

WITH proud thanksgiving, a mother for her children,
England mourns for her dead across the sea.
Flesh of her flesh they were, spirit of her spirit,
Fallen in the cause of the free.

Solemn the drums thrill: Death august and royal
Sings sorrow up into immortal spheres.
There is music in the midst of desolation
And a glory that shines upon our tears.

They went with songs to the battle, they were young,
Straight of limb, true of eye, steady and aglow.
They were staunch to the end against odds uncounted.
They fell with their faces to the foe.

They shall grow not old, as we that are left grow old;
Age shall not weary them, nor the years condemn.
At the going down of the sun and in the morning
We will remember them.

They mingle not with their laughing comrades again;
They sit no more at familiar tables of home;
They have no lot in our labour of the day-time;
They sleep beyond England's foam.

But where our desires are and our hopes profound,
Felt as a well-spring that is hidden from sight,
To the innermost heart of their own land they are known
As the stars are known to the Night;

As the stars that shall be bright when we are dust,
Moving in marches upon the heavenly plain,
As the stars that are starry in the time of our darkness,
To the end, to the end, they remain.

This poem, with its poignant associations with Remembrance Sunday and countless war memorials, was written shortly after the outbreak of war and was first published in *The Times* in September, 1914. That it is popularly supposed to have been written at the end of the war is not hard to understand, since it seems to offer consolation to a bereaved nation after years of slaughter, and its tone of pomp and circumstance suggests the Cenotaph and the ritual of a State occasion.

Its ceremonial manner and powerfully emotional appeal are

largely responsible for the enormous success of the poem. To a nation growing numbed by the mounting and unprecedented casualty figures of the war it became a source of comfort and an anodyne to soothe public grief; for its incantatory movement, its evocative imagery, its glorification of death in battle and its idealization of the men who died, effectively transmute the ugliness and cruelty of war into an exultation of the human spirit, so that the horror becomes more tolerable.

Binyon had some knowledge of the reality of war—he served at the Front as a Red Cross orderly in 1916, and wrote poems based upon his experience there—but his most widely known poem lends a majesty and dignity to the suffering of the First World War that to other participants was incompatible with the facts.

SIEGFRIED SASSOON (1886–1967)

THE REDEEMER

DARKNESS: the rain sluiced down; the mire was deep;
It was past twelve on a mid-winter night,
When peaceful folk in beds lay snug asleep;
There, with much work to do before the light,
We lugged our clay-sucked boots as best we might
Along the trench; sometimes a bullet sang,
And droning shells burst with a hollow bang;
We were soaked, chilled and wretched, every one;
Darkness; the distant wink of a huge gun.

I turned in the black ditch, loathing the storm;
A rocket fizzed and burned with blanching flare,
And lit the face of what had been a form
Floundering in mirk. He stood before me there;

I say that He was Christ; stiff in the glare,
And leaning forward from His burdening task,
Both arms supporting it; His eyes on mine
Stared from the woeful head that seemed a mask
Of mortal pain in Hell's unholy shine.

No thorny crown, only a woollen cap
He wore—an English soldier, white and strong,
Who loved his time like any simple chap,
Good days of work and sport and homely song;
Now he has learned that nights are very long,
And dawn a watching of the windowed sky.
But to the end, unjudging, he'll endure
Horror and pain, not uncontent to die
That Lancaster on Lune may stand secure.

He faced me, reeling in his weariness,
Shouldering his load of planks, so hard to bear.
I say that He was Christ, who wrought to bless
All groping things with freedom bright as air,
And with His mercy washed and made them fair.
Then the flame sank, and all grew black as pitch,
While we began to struggle along the ditch;
And someone flung his burden in the muck,
Mumbling: "O Christ Almighty, now I'm stuck!"

SUICIDE IN THE TRENCHES

I KNEW a simple soldier boy
Who grinned at life in empty joy,
Slept soundly through the lonesome dark,
And whistled early with the lark.

In winter trenches, cowed and glum,
With crumps and lice and lack of rum,
He put a bullet through his brain.
No one spoke of him again.

You smug-faced crowds with kindling eye
Who cheer when soldier lads march by,
Sneak home and pray you'll never know
The hell where youth and laughter go.

MEMORIAL TABLET

(Great War, 1918)

SQUIRE nagged and bullied till I went to fight
(Under Lord Derby's scheme). I died in hell—
(They called it Passchendaele); my wound was slight,
And I was hobbling back, and then a shell
Burst slick upon the duck-boards; so I fell
Into the bottomless mud, and lost the light.

In sermon-time, while Squire is in his pew,
He gives my gilded name a thoughtful stare;
For though low down upon the list, I'm there:
"In proud and glorious memory"—that's my due.
Two bleeding years I fought in France for Squire;
I suffered anguish that he's never guessed;
Once I came home on leave; and then went west.
What greater glory could a man desire?

Siegfried Sassoon was the first of the poets of the Great War
with direct experience of the trenches to write outspokenly in
denunciation of what the soldier had to endure, and the first
publicly to accuse the authorities of sacrificing men's lives by

deliberately prolonging the war. The desperate courage that such a stand required might not have been suspected in the young fox-hunting man whose gentlemanly way of life was shattered in 1914, but it was another aspect of the physical courage which earned him the nickname of "Mad Jack" in the front line, and with which he won the Military Cross.

In these poems is heard for the first time the authentic voice of the ordinary, unheroic soldier, for Sassoon, like Wilfred Owen, wrote on behalf of the inarticulate many. In *The Redeemer*, the laborious misery of the detachment shoring up the trench walls is suddenly illuminated by the vision of the Christ-figure: the soldier with his burden of wood is momentarily seen as the Saviour, come "to bless All groping things". But the flare subsides, the Redeemer reverts to the role of the common soldier who is prepared to die for others, and the return to reality is emphasized by the calculated blasphemy of the last line.

Suicide in the Trenches is an example of the controlled anger Sassoon could command. After the deliberately simple style and verse form of the opening, the act of suicide in the seventh line comes as a shock for which we are unprepared, and the full onslaught of biting contempt in the last verse produces a climax which makes Sassoon's point with tremendous force and effectiveness.

In *Memorial Tablet* we are similarly unprepared for the climax, for the opening lines seem to give an almost nonchalant account of recruitment and death, followed by four lines of apparently quiet reflection on the church plaque; but then the change of mood begins to assert itself ("Two bleeding years . . .") and the bitterness rises to the culminating irony of "What greater glory could a man desire?"

Sassoon's ability to identify himself with the ordinary fighting man, and to express his anger and hopelessness in a convincing colloquial idiom deliberately designed to shock the complacent, gave a new vigour to war poetry which made the old heroics sound hollow and unreal.

Edward Thomas (1878–1917)

THIS IS NO CASE OF PETTY RIGHT
OR WRONG

This is no case of petty right or wrong
That politicians or philosophers
Can judge. I hate not Germans, nor grow hot
With love of Englishmen, to please newspapers.
Beside my hate for one fat patriot
My hatred of the Kaiser is love true:—
A kind of god he is, banging a gong.
But I have not to choose between the two,
Or between justice and injustice. Dinned
With war and argument I read no more
Than in the storm smoking along the wind
Athwart the wood. Two witches' cauldrons roar.
From one the weather shall rise clear and gay;
Out of the other an England beautiful
And like her mother that died yesterday.
Little I know or care if, being dull,
I shall miss something that historians
Can rake out of the ashes when perchance
The phoenix broods serene above their ken.
But with the best and meanest Englishmen
I am one in crying, God save England, lest
We lose what never slaves and cattle blessed.
The ages made her that made us from the dust:
She is all we know and live by, and we trust
She is good and must endure, loving her so:
And as we love ourselves we hate her foe.

A PRIVATE

THIS ploughman dead in battle slept out of doors
Many a frozen night, and merrily
Answered staid drinkers, good bedmen, and all bores:
"At Mrs. Greenland's Hawthorn Bush," said he,
"I slept." None knew which bush. Above the town,
Beyond "The Drover", a hundred spot the down
In Wiltshire. And where now at last he sleeps
More sound in France—that, too, he secret keeps.

Edward Thomas, who was killed in action at Arras in 1917,
wrote little about the war and is better known for his poems of
rural life, which he treated with acute perceptiveness and in a
quiet, personal style beneath which lies a feeling of strength and
uncompromising honesty.

The two poems quoted here illustrate some of these qualities,
and, although both can be called "war poems", each has its
allusion to the English countryside as a significant feature of its
total effect; for although Thomas was a poet in uniform, he
retained an attitude of reserve about the war which owed much
to his depth of feeling for the country life he knew best.

In *This Is No Case of Petty Right or Wrong*, he reaches a con-
clusion about patriotism which we feel is valid because it has been
arrived at by a process of clear-sighted truthfulness—one which
may make Brooke's *The Soldier* appear comparatively facile; for
Thomas dismisses the wartime propaganda and concentrates
upon what he himself holds to be good and of lasting value.

The same independence of spirit is present in *A Private*, where
the ploughman's self-sufficiency is maintained even in death; and
the respect that Thomas feels is due to the man is reflected in the
laconic tone of the poem.

Thomas did not make the protests about war that we associate

with poets like Sassoon and Owen, but the sanity and integrity
exhibited in these poems, although less dramatic, have a peculiar
value of their own.

WILFRED OWEN (1893–1918)

THE PARABLE OF THE OLD MEN
AND THE YOUNG

So ABRAM rose, and clave the wood, and went,
And took the fire with him, and a knife.
And as they sojourned both of them together,
Isaac the first-born spake and said, My Father,
Behold the preparations, fire and iron,
But where the lamb for this burnt-offering?
Then Abram bound the youth with belts and straps,
And builded parapets and trenches there,
And stretchèd forth the knife to slay his son.
When lo! an angel called him out of heaven,
Saying, Lay not thy hand upon the lad,
Neither do anything to him. Behold,
A ram, caught in a thicket by its horns;
Offer the Ram of Pride instead of him.
But the old man would not so, but slew his son,—
And half the seed of Europe, one by one.

INSENSIBILITY

I

HAPPY are men who yet before they are killed
Can let their veins run cold.
Whom no compassion fleers
Or makes their feet
Sore on the alleys cobbled with their brothers.
The front line withers,
But they are troops who fade, not flowers
For poets' tearful fooling:
Men, gaps for filling:
Losses who might have fought
Longer; but no one bothers.

II

And some cease feeling
Even themselves or for themselves.
Dullness best solves
The tease and doubt of shelling,
And Chance's strange arithmetic
Comes simpler than the reckoning of their shilling.
They keep no check on armies' decimation.

III

Happy are these who lose imagination:
They have enough to carry with ammunition.
Their spirit drags no pack,
Their old wounds save with cold can not more ache.
Having seen all things red,
Their eyes are rid
Of the hurt of the colour of blood for ever.
And terror's first constriction over,
Their hearts remain small-drawn.

Their senses in some scorching cautery of battle
Now long since ironed,
Can laugh among the dying, unconcerned.

IV

Happy the soldier home, with not a notion
How somewhere, every dawn, some men attack,
And many sighs are drained.
Happy the lad whose mind was never trained:
His days are worth forgetting more than not.
He sings along the march
Which we march taciturn, because of dusk,
The long, forlorn, relentless tread
From larger day to huger night.

V

We wise, who with a thought besmirch
Blood over all our soul,
How should we see our task
But through his blunt and lashless eyes?
Alive, he is not vital overmuch;
Dying, not mortal overmuch;
Nor sad, nor proud,
Nor curious at all.
He cannot tell
Old men's placidity from his.

VI

But cursed are dullards whom no cannon stuns,
That they should be as stones;
Wretched are they, and mean
With paucity that never was simplicity.
By choice they made themselves immune
To pity and whatever moans in man
Before the last sea and the hapless stars;
Whatever mourns when many leave these shores;
Whatever shares
The eternal reciprocity of tears.

SPRING OFFENSIVE

HALTING against the shade of a last hill,
They fed, and, lying easy, were at ease
And, finding comfortable chests and knees,
Carelessly slept. But many there stood still
To face the stark, blank sky beyond the ridge,
Knowing their feet had come to the end of the world.

Marvelling they stood, and watched the long grass swirled
By the May breeze, murmurous with wasp and midge,
For though the summer oozed into their veins
Like an injected drug for their bodies' pains,
Sharp on their souls hung the imminent line of grass,
Fearfully flashed the sky's mysterious glass.

Hour after hour they ponder the warm field—
And the far valley behind, where the buttercup
Had blessed with gold their slow boots coming up,
Where even the little brambles would not yield,
But clutched and clung to them like sorrowing hands;
They breathe like trees unstirred.

Till like a cold gust thrills the little word
At which each body and its soul begird
And tighten them for battle. No alarms
Of bugles, no high flags, no clamorous haste—
Only a lift and flare of eyes that faced
The sun, like a friend with whom their love is done.
O larger shone that smile against the sun,—
Mightier than his whose bounty these have spurned.

So, soon they topped the hill, and raced together
Over an open stretch of herb and heather
Exposed. And instantly the whole sky burned

With fury against them; earth set sudden cups
In thousands for their blood; and the green slope
Chasmed and steepened sheer to infinite space.

.   .   .   .   .   .

Of them who running on that last high place
Leapt to swift unseen bullets, or went up
On the hot blast and fury of hell's upsurge,
Or plunged and fell away past this world's verge,
Some say God caught them even before they fell.

But what say such as from existence' brink
Ventured but drave too swift to sink,
The few who rushed in the body to enter hell,
And there out-fiending all its fiends and flames
With superhuman inhumanities,
Long-famous glories, immemorial shames—
And crawling slowly back, have by degrees
Regained cool peaceful air in wonder—
Why speak not they of comrades that went under?

ANTHEM FOR DOOMED YOUTH

WHAT passing-bells for these who die as cattle?
    Only the monstrous anger of the guns.
    Only the stuttering rifles' rapid rattle
Can patter out their hasty orisons.
No mockeries for them from prayers or bells,
    Nor any voice of mourning save the choirs,—
The shrill, demented choirs of wailing shells;
    And bugles calling for them from sad shires.

What candles may be held to speed them all?
    Not in the hands of boys, but in their eyes
Shall shine the holy glimmers of good-byes.
    The pallor of girls' brows shall be their pall;
Their flowers the tenderness of silent minds,
And each slow dusk a drawing-down of blinds.

THE END

AFTER the blast of lightning from the East,
The flourish of loud clouds, the Chariot Throne;
After the drums of Time have rolled and ceased,
And by the bronze west long retreat is blown,

Shall life renew these bodies? Of a truth
All death will He annul, all tears assuage?—
Fill the void veins of Life again with youth,
And wash, with an immortal water, Age?

When I do ask white Age he saith not so:
"My head hangs weighed with snow."
And when I hearken to the Earth, she saith:
"My fiery heart shrinks, aching. It is death.
Mine ancient scars shall not be glorified,
Nor my titanic tears, the sea, be dried."

Wilfred Owen, who was killed in action one week before the Armistice in 1918, is generally regarded as the best of the poets of the First World War. When he was still a boy he had the firm ambition to become a poet, but it was only when he had experienced the horrors of the war that he quite suddenly seemed to find the maturity of expression that his best poems exhibit, for all his finest verse was composed in the last few years of his life, and much of it in the last few months.

Like Sassoon, whom he knew, and for whom he had a tremendous admiration, Owen wished to speak out clearly on behalf of the men who were suffering in the trenches; but while he was capable of anger and a powerful indignation at the outrages he witnessed and at the apparent indifference of those in authority, the source of his inspiration was more frequently a compassion for the sufferers—enemies as well as friends—and a deeply felt sense of the appalling wastefulness of war in terms not only of the physical casualties but of the human spirit.

In *The Parable of the Old Men and the Young* Owen takes the

story of God's testing of Abraham's faith (Genesis, 22), and turns
it into an allegory showing how the older generation was pre-
pared to sacrifice the younger in the interest of pride. The
effectiveness of the poem lies in its use of a rather staid blank-
verse line, in which hints of a military nature are inserted into
the predominantly biblical language, leading suddenly to a
climax in which a violent twist is given to the Bible story's
ending, in a rhyming couplet which not only clinches the poem's
point but, with its juxtaposition of "half the seed of Europe" and
"one by one", suggests the deaths of millions as separate and cal-
culated acts of murder.

The restraint with which this horrifying conclusion is reached
is characteristic of Owen's best poetry. In *Insensibility* the ironic
conception of the soldier's "happiness" resulting from the deaden-
ing of his response to slaughter and fear is expressed in deliberate,
measured language which remains under perfect control even
when the upsurge of angry bitterness is released in the last
stanza, with its majestic and memorable conclusion. The total
effect of the poem is enhanced by Owen's use of assonantal
rhyme with its suggestiveness of a dulled melancholy, and by the
subtly modulated rhythms which illustrate the poet's perfect con-
trol over his material.

Spring Offensive is a brilliant account of the tension of men
about to go into action. The apparent calm of the opening
stanzas is belied by allusions to fear and anxiety: the awareness of
danger is set in ironic contrast to the beauty of the scene. The
powerful climax describing the violence of the attack marks the
release of tension, the lines gathering momentum as "the ridge"
and "the imminent line of grass" of the earlier stanzas becomes
"the green slope" which "chasmed and steepened sheer to
infinite space", with its physical sense of headlong falling. The
last section builds up to a second climax which continues the
theme of violence and then re-establishes a kind of tranquillity by
its compassionate tone, but the final question suggests a return
to a mood similar to the anxiety of the opening, leaving a feeling
of profound disquiet.

The sonnet, *Anthem For Doomed Youth*, shows Owen's capacity for expressing a mood of angry bitterness which passes subtly into an elegaic mood of compassion. Most of the octet is concerned with a harsh, sardonic contrast between the funeral rites of a peaceful burial service and the circumstances of death on the battlefield, but in its final line the tone softens, and, by means of a skilfully contrived link, the sestet continues in a gentler manner, still retaining the original contrast, but with the bitterness gone, and concluding with an image of perfect and moving aptness.

A more rhetorical tone is evident in *The End*, with its apocalyptic echoes (see Revelation, especially Chapters 4 and 5), but even in the tragic pessimism of this poem the mood is essentially compassionate, and exemplifies the theme of "pity" which runs throughout Owen's poetry.

Owen's greatness lies in his ability not only to present the sufferings of men in war with fierce realism, but to invest his account of war with intense moral feeling, and, in language of notable originality, to set it in a context in which both human and spiritual values are of significance.

G. K. Chesterton (1874–1936)

ELEGY IN A COUNTRY CHURCHYARD

> The men that worked for England
> They have their graves at home;
> And bees and birds of England
> About the cross can roam.
>
> But they that fought for England,
> Following a falling star,
> Alas, alas for England
> They have their graves afar.

> And they that rule in England,
> In stately conclave met,
> Alas, alas for England
> They have no graves as yet.

Chesterton, with his celebrated hatred of cant and hypocrisy, reached the same conclusion as some of the men in the trenches: that the rulers of England had much to answer for in their conduct of the war.

The suggestion of decent restraint implied in the title's allusion to Gray's *Elegy* is fulfilled in the conventional tone of the first two stanzas, so that one is unprepared for the thrust that is made at respectability in the final lines. This poem lacks the intensity of feeling, arising from cruel experience, that one finds in Sassoon and Owen, but it makes its point shrewdly.

REX WARNER (BORN 1905)

ARMS IN SPAIN

So THAT men might remain slaves, and that the little good
they hoped for might be turned all bad and the iron lie
stamped and clamped on growing tender and vigorous truth
these machine-guns were despatched from Italy.

So that the drunken General and the Christian millionaire
might continue blindly to rule in complete darkness,
that on rape and ruin order might be founded firm,
these guns were sent to save civilization.

Lest the hand should be held at last more valuable than paper,
lest man's body and mind should be counted more than gold,
lest love should blossom, not shells, and break in the land
these machine-guns came from Christian Italy.

And to root out reason, lest hope be held in it,
to turn love inward into corroding hate,
lest men should be men, for the bank-notes and the mystery
these guns, these tanks, these gentlemanly words.

STEPHEN SPENDER (BORN 1909)

ULTIMA RATIO REGUM*

THE guns spell money's ultimate reason
In letters of lead on the spring hillside.
But the boy lying dead under the olive trees
Was too young and too silly
To have been notable to their important eye.
He was a better target for a kiss.

When he lived, tall factory hooters never summoned him.
Nor did restaurant plate-glass doors revolve to wave him in.
His name never appeared in the papers.
The world maintained its traditional wall
Round the dead with their gold sunk deep as a well,
Whilst his life, intangible as a Stock Exchange rumour,
        drifted outside.

O too lightly he threw down his cap
One day when the breeze threw petals from the trees.
The unflowering wall sprouted with guns,
Machine-gun anger quickly scythed the grasses;
Flags and leaves fell from hands and branches;
The tweed cap rotted in the nettles.

---

* A reference to war as "the final argument of rulers".

Consider his life which was valueless
In terms of employment, hotel ledgers, news files.
Consider. One bullet in ten thousand kills a man.
Ask. Was so much expenditure justified
On the death of one so young and so silly
Lying under the olive trees, O world, O death?

C. DAY LEWIS (BORN 1904)

THE NABARA

*"They preferred, because of the rudeness of their heart, to die rather than
to surrender."*

Phase One

FREEDOM is more than a word, more than the base coinage
Of statesmen, the tyrant's dishonoured cheque, or the
    dreamer's mad
Inflated currency. She is mortal, we know, and made
In the image of simple men who have no taste for carnage
But sooner kill and are killed than see that image betrayed.
Mortal she is, yet rising always refreshed from her ashes:
She is bound to earth, yet she flies as high as a passage bird
To home wherever man's heart with seasonal warmth is
    stirred:
Innocent is her touch as the dawn's, but still it unleashes
The ravisher shades of envy. Freedom is more than a word.

I see man's heart two-edged, keen both for death and creation.
As a sculptor rejoices, stabbing and mutilating the stone
Into a shaplier life, and the two joys make one—
So man is wrought in his hour of agony and elation
To efface the flesh to reveal the crying need of his bone.

Burning the issue was beyond their mild forecasting
For those I tell of—men used to the tolerable joy and hurt
Of simple lives: they coveted never an epic part;
But history's hand was upon them and hewed an everlasting
Image of freedom out of their rude and stubborn heart.

The year, Nineteen-thirty-seven: month, March: the men,
    descendants
Of those Iberian fathers, the inquiring ones who would go
Wherever the sea-ways led: a pacific people, slow
To feel ambition, loving their laws and their independence—
Men of the Basque country, the Mar Cantábrico.
Fishermen, with no guile outside their craft, they had weathered
Often the sierra-ranked Biscayan surges, the wet
Fog of the Newfoundland Banks: they were fond of *pelota*:
    they met
No game beyond their skill as they swept the sea together,
Until the morning they found the leviathan in their net.

Government trawlers *Nabara, Guipuzkoa, Bizkaya,*
Donostia, escorting across blockaded seas
Galdames with her cargo of nickel and refugees
From Bayonne to Bilbao, while the crest of war curled higher
Inland over the glacial valleys, the ancient ease.
On the morning of March the fifth, a chill North-Wester
    fanned them,
Fogging the glassy waves: what uncharted doom lay low
There in the fog athwart their course, they could not know:
Stout were the armed trawlers, redoubtable those who
    manned them—
Men of the Basque country, the Mar Cantábrico.

Slowly they nosed ahead, while under the chill North-Wester
Nervous the sea crawled and twitched like the skin of a beast
That dreams of the chase, the kill, the blood-beslavered feast:
They too, the light-hearted sailors, dreamed of a fine fiesta,

Flags and their children waving, when they won home from
    the east.
Vague as images seen in a misted glass or the vision
Of crystal-gazer, the ships huddled, receded, neared,
Threading the weird fog-maze that coiled their funnels and
    bleared
Day's eye. They were glad of the fog till *Galdames* lost position
—Their convoy, precious in life and metal—and disappeared.

But still they held their course, the confident ear-ringed
    captains,
Unerring towards the landfall, nor guessed how the land lay,
How the guardian fog was a guide to lead them all astray.
For now, at a wink, the mist rolled up like a film that curtains
A saurian's eye; and into the glare of an evil day
Bizkaya, Guipuzkoa, Nabara, and the little
Donostia stepped at intervals; and sighted, alas,
Blocking the sea and sky a mountain they might not pass,
An isle thrown up volcanic and smoking, a giant in metal
Astride their path—the rebel cruiser, *Canarias*.

A ship of ten thousand tons she was, a heavyweight fighter
To the cocky bantam trawlers: and under her armament
Of eight- and four-inch guns there followed obedient
Towards Pasajes a prize just seized, an Estonian freighter
Laden with arms the exporters of death to Spain had sent.
A hush, the first qualm of conflict, falls on the cruiser's
    burnished
Turrets, the trawlers' grimy decks: fiercer the lime-
Light falls, and out of the solemn ring the late mists climb,
And ship to ship the antagonists gaze at each other
    astonished
Across the quaking gulf of the sea for a moment's time.

The trawlers' men had no chance or wish to elude the fated
Encounter. Freedom to these was natural pride that runs
Hot as the blood, their climate and heritage, dearer than sons.

Bizkaya, Guipuzkoa, knowing themselves outweighted,
Drew closer to draw first blood with their pairs of four-inch
      guns.
Aboard *Canarias* the German gun-layers stationed
Brisk at their intricate batteries—guns and men both trained
To a hair in accuracy, aimed at a pitiless end—
Fired, and the smoke rolled forth over the unimpassioned
Face of a day where nothing certain but death remained.

Phase Two

The sound of the first salvo skimmed the ocean and thumped
Cape Machichaco's granite ribs: it rebounded where
The salt-sprayed trees grow tough from wrestling the wind:
      it jumped
From isle to rocky isle: it was heard by women while
They walked to shrine or market, a warning they must fear.
But, beyond their alarm, as
Though that sound were also a signal for fate to strip
Luck's last green shoot from the falling stock of the Basques,
      Galdames
Emerged out of the mist that lingered to the west
Under the reeking muzzles of the rebel battleship:

Which instantly threw five shells over her funnel, and threw
Her hundred women and children into a slaughter-yard panic
On the deck they imagined smoking with worse than the foggy
      dew,
So that *Galdames* rolled as they slipped, clawed, trampled,
      reeled
Away from the gape of the cruiser's guns. A spasm galvanic,
Fear's chemistry, shocked the women's bodies, a moment before
Huddled like sheep in a mist, inert as bales of rag,
A mere deck-cargo: but more
Than furies now, for they stormed *Galdames'* bridge and
      swarmed
Over her captain and forced him to run up the white flag.

Signalling the Estonian, "Heave-to", *Canarias* steamed
Leisurely over to make sure of this other prize:
Over-leisurely was her reckoning—she never dreamed
The Estonian in that pause could be snatched from her
    shark-shape jaws
By ships of minnow size.
Meanwhile *Nabara* and *Guipuzkoa*, not reluctant
For closer grips while their guns and crews were still entire,
Thrust forward: twice *Guipuzkoa* with a deadly jolt was
    rocked, and
The sea spat up in geysers of boiling foam, as the cruiser's
Heavier guns boxed them in a torrid zone of fire.

And now the little *Donostia* who lay with her 75's
Dumb in the offing—her weapons against that leviathan
Impotent as pen-knives—
Witnessed a bold manoeuvre, a move of genius, never
In naval history told. She saw *Bizkaya* run
Ahead of her consorts, a beserk atom of steel, audacious,
Her signal flags soon to flutter like banderillas, straight
Towards the Estonian speeding, a young bull over the
    spacious
And foam-distraught arena, till the sides of the freight-ship
    screen her
From *Canarias* that will see the point of her charge too late.

"Who are you and where are you going?" the flags of
    Bizkaya questioned.
"Carrying arms and forced to go to Pasajes," replied
The Estonian. "Follow me to harbour." "Cannot, am
    threatened."
Bizkaya's last word—"Turn at once!"—and she points her
    peremptory guns
Against the freighter's mountainous flanks that blankly hide
This fluttering language and flaunt of signal insolence
From the eyes of *Canarias*. At last the rebels can see

That the two ships' talk meant a practical joke at their
    expense:
They see the Estonian veering away, to Bermeo steering,
Bizkaya under her lee.

(To the Basques that ship was a tonic, for she carried some
    million rounds
Of ammunition: to hearts grown sick with hope deferred
And the drain of their country's wounds
She brought what most they needed in face of the aid
    evaded
And the cold delay of those to whom freedom was only
    a word.)*
Owlish upon the water sat the *Canarias*
Mobbed by those darting trawlers, and her signals blinked
    in vain
After the freighter, that still she believed too large to pass
Into Bermeo's port—a prize she fondly thought,
When she'd blown the trawlers out of the water, she'd take
    again.

Brisk at their intricate batteries the German gun-layers go
About death's business, knowing their longer reach must foil
The impetus, break the heart of the government ships: each
    blow
Deliberately they aim, and tiger-striped with flame
Is the jungle mirk of the smoke as their guns leap and recoil.

---

* Cf. Byron's comments upon "Non-Intervention" in *The Age of Bronze*:

> Lone, lost, abandoned in their utmost need
> By Christians, unto whom they gave their creed,
> The desolated lands, the ravaged isle,
> The fostered feud encouraged to beguile,
> The aid evaded, and the cold delay
> Prolonged but in the hope to make a prey:
> These, these shall tell the tale, and Greece can show
> The false friend worse than the infuriate foe.

(Mr. Day Lewis's note)

The Newfoundland trawlers feel
A hail and hurricane the like they have never known
In all their deep-sea life: they wince at the squalls of steel
That burst on their open decks, rake them and leave them
    wrecks,
But still they fight on long into the sunless afternoon.

—Fought on, four guns against the best of the rebel navy,
Until *Guipuzkoa's* crew could stanch the fires no more
That gushed from her gashes and seeped nearer the magazine.
    Heavy
At heart they turned away for the Nervion that day:
Their ship, *Guipuzkoa*, wore
Flame's rose on her heart like a decoration of highest honour
As listing she reeled into Las Arenas; and in a row
On her deck there lay, smoke-palled, that oriflamme's crackling
    banner
Above them, her dead—a quarter of the fishermen who had
    fought her—
Men of the Basque country, the Mar Cantábrico.

Phase Three

And now the gallant *Nabara* was left in the ring alone,
The sky hollow around her, the fawning sea at her side:
But the ear-ringed crew in their berets stood to the guns,
    and cried
A fresh defiance down
The ebb of the afternoon, the battle's darkening tide.
Honour was satisfied long since, they had held and harried
A ship ten times their size; they well could have called it
    a day.
But they hoped, if a little longer they kept the cruiser in
    play,
Galdames with the wealth of life and metal she carried
Might make her getaway.

Canarias, though easily she outpaced and out-gunned her,
Finding this midge could sting
Edged off, and beneath a wedge of smoke steamed in a ring
On the rim of the trawler's range, a circular storm of thunder.
But always *Nabara* turned her broadside, manoeuvering
To keep both guns on the target, scorning safety devices.
Slower now battle's tempo, irregular the beat
Of gunfire in the heart
Of the afternoon, the distempered sky sank to the crisis,
Shell-shocked the sea tossed and hissed in delirious heat.

The battle's tempo slowed, for the cruiser could take her time,
And the guns of *Nabara* grew
Red-hot, and of fifty-two Basque seamen had been her crew
Many were dead already, the rest filthy with grime
And their comrades' blood, weary with wounds all but a few.
Between two fires they fought, for the sparks that flashing spoke
From the cruiser's thunder-bulk were answered on their own
        craft
By traitor flames that crawled out of every cranny and rift
Blinding them all with smoke.
At half-past four *Nabara* was burning fore and aft.

What buoyancy of will
Was theirs to keep her afloat, no vessel now but a sieve—
So jarred and scarred, the rivets starting, no inch of her safe
From the guns of the foe that wrapped her in a cyclone of
        shrieking steel!
Southward the sheltering havens showed clear, the cliffs and
        the surf
Familiar to them from childhood, the shapes of a life still dear:
But dearer still to see
Those shores insured for life from the shadow of tyranny.
Freedom was not on their lips; it was what made them
        endure,
A steel spring in the yielding flesh, a thirst to be free.

And now from the little *Donostia* that lay with her 75's
Dumb in the offing, they saw *Nabara* painfully lower
A boat, which crawled like a shattered crab slower and slower
Towards them. They cheered the survivors, thankful to save
    these lives
At least. They saw each rower,
As the boat dragged alongside, was wounded—the oars they
    held
Dripping with blood, a bloody skein reeled out in their wake:
And they swarmed down the rope-ladders to rescue these men
    so weak
From wounds they must be hauled
Aboard like babies. And then they saw they had made a
    mistake.

For, standing up in the boat,
A man in that grimy boat's-crew hailed them: "Our
    officer asks
You give us your bandages and all your water-casks,
Then run for Bermeo. We're going to finish this game of
    pelota."
Donostia's captain begged them with tears to escape: but the
    Basques
Would play their game to the end.
They took the bandages, and cursing at his delay
They took the casks that might keep the fires on their ship
    at bay;
And they rowed back to *Nabara*, trailing their blood behind
Over the water, the sunset and crimson ebb of their day.

For two hours more they fought, while *Nabara* beneath their feet
Was turned to a heap of smouldering scrap-iron. Once again
The flames they had checked a while broke out. When the
    forward gun
Was hit, they turned about
Bringing the after gun to bear. They fought in pain

And the instant knowledge of death: but the waters filling their
    riven
Ship could not quench the love that fired them. As each man
    fell
To the deck, his body took fire as if death made visible
That burning spirit. For two more hours they fought, and
    at seven
They fired their last shell.

Of her officers all but one were dead. Of her engineers
All but one were dead. Of the fifty-two that had sailed
In her, all were dead but fourteen—and each of these half
    killed
With wounds. And the night-dew fell in a hush of ashen
    tears,
And *Nabara's* tongue was stilled.
Southward the sheltering havens grew dark, the cliffs and the
    green
Shallows they knew; where their friends had watched them
    as evening wore
To a glowing end, who swore
Nabara must show a white flag now, but saw instead the
    fourteen
Climb into their matchwood boat and fainting pull for
    the shore.

Canarias lowered a launch that swept in a greyhound's curve
Pitiless to pursue
And cut them off. But that bloodless and all-but-phantom crew
Still gave no soft concessions to fate: they strung their nerve
For one last fling of defiance, they shipped their oars and threw
Hand-grenades at the launch as it circled about to board them.
But the strength of the hands that had carved them a hold
    on history
Failed them at last: the grenades fell short of the enemy,
Who grappled and overpowered them,
While *Nabara* sank by the stern in the hushed Cantabrian sea.

They bore not a charmed life. They went into battle
    foreseeing
Probable loss, and they lost. The tides of Biscay flow
Over the obstinate bones of many, the winds are sighing
Round prison walls where the rest are doomed like their
    ship to rust—
Men of the Basque country, the Mar Cantábrico.
Simple men who asked of their life no mythical splendour,
They loved its familiar ways so well that they preferred
In the rudeness of their heart to die rather than to surrender . . .
Mortal these words and the deed they remember, but cast
    a seed
Shall flower for an age when freedom is man's creative word.

Freedom was more than a word, more than the base coinage
Of politicians who hiding behind the skirts of peace
They had defiled, gave up that country to rack and carnage:
For whom, indelibly stamped with history's contempt,
Remains but to haunt the blackened shell of their policies.
For these I have told of, freedom was flesh and blood—
    a mortal
Body, the gun-breech hot to its touch: yet the battle's
    height
Raised it to love's meridian and held it awhile immortal;
And its light through time still flashes like a star's that has
    turned to ashes,
Long after *Nabara's* passion was quenched in the sea's heart.

The Spanish Civil War (1936–9), which is the subject of these
poems by Rex Warner, Stephen Spender and C. Day Lewis, was
seen by many people at the time as a preparation for the wider
conflict they expected would come between the forces of fascism
and capitalism and those of democratic socialism and commun-
ism. For this reason it engaged the attention, and sometimes the
active participation—usually in the International Brigade—of
intellectuals from countries not directly involved in the war.

General Franco's rebellion against the Spanish left-wing govern-
ment led to nearly three years of savage fighting, during which
the insurgents were supplied with arms and volunteers from
Hitler's Germany and Mussolini's Italy, while democratic
governments, including the British, pursued a policy of "non-
intervention", an attitude which earned the bitter contempt of
those who saw the war as a threat to democracy and liberty.

These three poems reflect some of the intense feeling that the
war aroused in the minds of some of the "committed" writers at
that time. Rex Warner's *Arms in Spain* expresses most clearly the
burning anger engendered in those who hated fascism. He sees
the war as a conflict between good and evil, in which freedom,
truth, love and human dignity are being destroyed by those who
pretend to uphold "civilization" and Christianity. Although the
heavily ironic tone of the poem becomes at times rather exag-
gerated, the general effect is of a controlled invective, and
Warner found here a verse-form which exactly suited the mood
of smouldering rage that the political situation evoked in him and
in many who shared his sympathies.

Stephen Spender's *Ultima Ratio Regum* uses more subtle means
to arouse sympathy. He appears, at first sight, to be less "in-
volved" than Warner (although Spender in fact went to Spain as
a government supporter); but by singling out one incident of
death, and by using a gentler manner and a less obtrusive form of
irony, he makes quite clear which side he is on. The irony lies in
the attempt to see the dead boy's value in terms of economics, for
in these terms he is unimportant, and unworthy of the expenditure
involved in having him killed. By stressing the insignificance of
the boy as the capitalist world might see him, Spender implies his
worth as assessed in human values: and it is as a plea on behalf of
those values that the poem, in spite of a rather self-conscious
manner, may be judged.

C. Day Lewis's *The Nabara* is one of the best narrative poems of
our time. Based upon an episode related in G. L. Steer's *The Tree
of Gernika*, it is one of the few examples of a successful attempt to
give heroic treatment to a twentieth-century battle. In some

respects it is interesting to compare the poem with *The Defence of Lucknow* (p. 68), in which a similar metrical pattern is used, but *The Nabara* avoids the ponderousness of Tennyson's poem and, in comparison, has an almost lyrical quality about it. This is due partly to Day Lewis's use of a more varied rhyme-scheme (including the use of assonantal rhyme), incorporated in regular ten-line stanzas, but mainly to his much more imaginative use of language, with its powerful imagery, in which he combines the rhetorical with the colloquial in a remarkably successful synthesis. The frequency of run-on lines, too, gives a feeling of urgency to the story, so that a tension is built up between the rhythm of the metrical beat and that of the grammatical construction. The sense of the heroic that Day Lewis creates in this poem is, of course, related to the same partisan attitude to the Spanish Civil War which moved Warner and Spender, but the poem rises above the immediate circumstances of its composition because it is a tribute to the obstinate courage and defiance of a David pitting his inadequate strength against a Goliath, a situation which will always have an appeal.

All three of these poems are poems of protest, and may still be regarded by some as pieces of propaganda, since they see a comparatively recent war in terms of black and white, of good versus evil; but a great deal of war poetry must necessarily be of this kind: the Frenchmen in *Henry V* are stupidly arrogant, Dryden's Dutchmen are "bold in others, not themselves", and Tennyson's Indian rebels are "murderous". It may be possible in years to come to leave the war to the historians and assess the poetry on its own merits.

W. H. AUDEN (BORN 1907)

THE QUARRY

O WHAT is that sound which so thrills the ear
  Down in the valley drumming, drumming?
Only the scarlet soldiers, dear,
  The soldiers coming.

O what is that light I see flashing so clear
  Over the distance brightly, brightly?
Only the sun on their weapons, dear,
  As they step lightly.

O what are they doing with all that gear,
  What are they doing this morning, this morning?
Only their usual manoeuvres, dear,
  Or perhaps a warning.

O why have they left the road down there,
  Why are they suddenly wheeling, wheeling?
Perhaps a change in their orders, dear.
  Why are you kneeling?

O haven't they stopped for the doctor's care,
  Haven't they reined their horses, their horses?
Why, they are none of them wounded, dear,
  None of these forces.

O is it the parson they want, with white hair,
  Is it the parson, is it, is it?
No, they are passing his gateway, dear,
  Without a visit.

O it must be the farmer who lives so near.
  It must be the farmer so cunning, so cunning?
They have passed the farmyard already, dear,
  And now they are running.

O where are you going? Stay with me here!
  Were the vows you swore deceiving, deceiving?
No, I promised to love you, dear,
  But I must be leaving.

O it's broken the lock and splintered the door,
  O it's the gate where they're turning, turning;
Their boots are heavy on the floor
  And their eyes are burning.

W. H. Auden's poem is placed here because it "belongs" in the 1930's (Auden's poetry was at one time associated with that of Spender, Day Lewis and MacNeice, and he served in the Spanish Civil War); but its subject-matter has a quality of timelessness which makes its assignment to a period almost irrelevant. The feeling of menace that it so skilfully creates is achieved partly by the choice of stanza-form and metre, for the simple, ballad-like verse-form suggests an innocence and lightness and, simultaneously, by its drum-like beat, a hint of the threat to come. The question-and-answer pattern also contributes to the poem's effect, for the questions indicate a feeling of unease, mounting to a more insistent tone of anxiety and fear, while the reassurance of the answers becomes progressively less convincing. The climax of the last stanza suggests the unleashed violence and brutality that has been relentlessly moving towards its quarry throughout the poem, a menace that has been foreshadowed in the "scarlet" of the uniforms, the "flashing" weapons, and the "warning", of the first three stanzas. The unidentified nature of the speakers, the vagueness of the location, the references to the types of people—soldier, doctor, parson, farmer—all produce a deliberately generalized effect, so that the poem becomes an account of the threat, and implied realization, of military violence upon its innocent and frightened victim in any age, but perhaps with a special relevance to the experience and threat of that violence in the twentieth century.

TED HUGHES (BORN 1930)

SIX YOUNG MEN

THE celluloid of a photograph holds them well,—
Six young men, familiar to their friends.
Four decades that have faded and ochre-tinged
This photograph have not wrinkled the faces or the hands.
Though their cocked hats are not now fashionable,
Their shoes shine. One imparts an intimate smile,
One chews a grass, one lowers his eyes, bashful,
One is ridiculous with cocky pride—
Six months after this picture they were all dead.

All are trimmed for a Sunday jaunt. I know
That bilberried bank, that thick tree, that black wall,
Which are there yet and not changed. From where these sit
You hear the water of seven streams fall
To the roarer in the bottom, and through all
The leafy valley a rumouring of air go.
Pictured here, their expressions listen yet,
And still that valley has not changed its sound
Though their faces are four decades under the ground.

This one was shot in an attack and lay
Calling in the wire, then this one, his best friend,
Went out to bring him in and was shot too;
And this one, the very moment he was warned
From potting at tin-cans in no-man's-land,
Fell back dead with his rifle-sights shot away.
The rest, nobody knows what they came to,
But come to the worst they must have done, and held it
Closer than their hope; all were killed.

Here see a man's photograph,
The locket of a smile, turned overnight
Into the hospital of his mangled last
Agony and hours; see bundled in it
His mightier-than-a-man dead bulk and weight:
And on this one place which keeps him alive
(In his Sunday best) see fall war's worst
Thinkable flash and rending, onto his smile
Forty years rotting into soil.

That man's not more alive whom you confront
And shake by the hand, see hale, hear speak loud,
Than any of these six celluloid smiles are,
Nor prehistoric or fabulous beast more dead;
No thought so vivid as their smoking blood:
To regard this photograph might well dement,
Such contradictory permanent horrors here
Smile from the single exposure and shoulder out
One's own body from its instant and heat.

The striking quality of this poem is its compassion. Ted Hughes,
himself a young man when he wrote this in the 1950's, reaches
back to the First World War, through a photograph of six of its
victims, with a sympathy which brings the young men back to
life and at the same time laments the gulf of time which now
separates them from the living.

The first two stanzas introduce this contrast. By showing the
young men as they were when the photograph was taken, and the
concrete reality of the familiar place where it was taken, the
writer makes us feel a sympathy with the men and the scene, so
that both come physically alive; but each stanza ends with a
stark statement of the fact of death. The third stanza is con-
cerned, in equally realistic terms, with the manner of their
deaths. In the fourth stanza, past and present coalesce, for the
horror and violence of war are fused on to the familiar smile of
the photograph which the first two stanzas had made into a

living reality. The paradox of this fusion of life and death, past and present, is brought to a climax in the last stanza, for here the men are both alive in the immediate present and dead in a remote past; and the paradox is clinched in

> No thought so vivid as their smoking blood

The last four lines suggest the effect such reflections may produce: for the overwhelming horror which is finally recreated from the photograph may cause us to doubt the palpable warmth of our own physical being.

The diction of the poem combines a colloquial idiom with a powerful density of language and imagery which contribute to its tone of poignancy; and the skilfully wrought stanza-form, with its unobtrusive scheme of rhymes and half-rhymes, adds subtly to this effect. A memory of a past war is evoked here with an intense feeling of compassion which is both eloquent and moving.

The Second World War

It would be pretentious in this anthology to try to generalize about the poetry of the Second World War when only six of its poets are represented, and when some of the more significant names have been omitted, but there are characteristics common to much of the poetry of this period, and some reference to them may be useful in relating these poems to their predecessors.

It seemed to be taken for granted by these poets that there was no place for heroics or stirring patriotism, for the merely dramatic or the sentimental. Since war had become a condition of life in which almost everyone was involved, the false note and the theatrical gesture were generally rejected as inappropriate.

In contrast with many of the poems of both the First World War and the Spanish Civil War, there is an absence of bitterness and protest here, for such attitudes seemed inappropriate in a situation in which civilians at home shared the dangers of war with the men in the front line, and there was no need to arouse an ignorant or apathetic public opinion. Instead there was displayed a more personal attitude which reflected the individual's response to his alien environment and a determination to preserve a sense of balance and perspective in a world where such qualities were lacking.

The mechanized and scientific nature of modern war also left its mark on the poetry of this period, and perhaps contributed to the air of detachment notable in some of the verse represented here. When Percy met the Douglas 'they swakked their swords . . .", unlike the mathematically trained fighting man who can calculate the death of his enemy at a distance of many miles. This is not to suggest that all the poetry of the Second World War is impersonal, but that much of it seems to strive after a cool objectivity.

The Second World War poems which follow are not claimed to be completely representative, but they may provide some illustration of how that war was seen by a few of the men who in various situations experienced it.

HENRY REED (BORN 1914)

LESSONS OF THE WAR

(To Alan Mitchell)

Vixi duellis nuper idoneus
Et militavi non sine gloria

I. Naming of Parts

TODAY we have naming of parts. Yesterday,
We had daily cleaning. And tomorrow morning,
We shall have what to do after firing. But to-day,
To-day we have naming of parts. Japonica
Glistens like coral in all of the neighbouring gardens
        And today we have naming of parts.

This is the lower sling swivel. And this
Is the upper sling swivel, whose use you will see
When you are given your slings. And this is the piling swivel,
Which in your case you have not got. The branches
Hold in the gardens their silent, eloquent gestures,
     Which in our case we have not got.

This is the safety catch, which is always released
With an easy flick of the thumb. And please do not let me
See anyone using his finger. You can do it quite easy
If you have any strength in your thumb. The blossoms
Are fragile and motionless, never letting anyone see
     Any of them using their finger.

And this you can see is the bolt. The purpose of this
Is to open the breech, as you see. We can slide it
Rapidly backwards and forwards; we call this
Easing the spring. And rapidly backwards and forwards
The early bees are assaulting and fumbling the flowers:
     They call it easing the Spring.

They call it easing the Spring; it is perfectly easy
If you have any strength in your thumb: like the bolt,
And the breech, and the cocking-piece, and the point of
     balance,
Which in our case we have not got; and the almond blossom
Silent in all of the gardens and the bees going backwards and
     forwards,
     For to-day we have naming of parts.

II. Judging Distances

Not only how far away, but the way that you say it
Is very important. Perhaps you may never get
The knack of judging a distance, but at least you know
How to report on a landscape; the central sector,
The right of arc and that, which we had last Tuesday,
     And at least you know

That maps are of time, not place, as far as the army
Happens to be concerned—the reason being,
Is one which need not delay us. Again, you know
There are three kinds of tree, three only, the fir and the
        poplar,
And those which have bushy tops to; and lastly
        That things only seem to be things.

A barn is not called a barn, to put it more plainly,
Or a field in the distance, where sheep may be safely grazing.
You must never be over-sure. You must say, when reporting:
At five o'clock in the central sector is a dozen
Of what appear to be animals; whatever you do,
        Don't call the bleeders *sheep*.

I am sure that's quite clear; and suppose, for the sake of
        example,
The one at the end, asleep, endeavours to tell us
What he sees over there to the west, and how far away,
After first having come to attention. There to the west
Of the fields of summer the sun and the shadows bestow
        Vestments of purple and gold.

The still white dwellings are like a mirage in the heat,
And under the swaying elms a man and a woman
Lie gently together. Which is, perhaps, only to say
That there is a row of houses to the left of arc,
And that under some poplars a pair of what appear to be
        humans
        Appear to be loving.

Well, that for an answer, is what we might rightly call
Moderately satisfactory only, the reason being,
Is that two things have been omitted, and those are
        important.
The human beings, now: in what direction are they,
And how far away, would you say? And do not forget
        There may be dead ground in between.

There may be dead ground in between; and I may not have
　　got
The knack of judging a distance; I will only venture
A guess that perhaps between me and the apparent lovers
(Who, incidentally, appear by now to have finished,)
At seven o'clock from the houses, is roughly a distance
　　Of about one year and a half.

III. Unarmed Combat

In due course of course you will all be issued with
Your proper issue; but until tomorrow,
You can hardly be said to need it; and until that time,
We shall have unarmed combat. I shall teach you
The various holds and rolls and throws and breakfalls
　　Which you may sometimes meet.

And the various holds and rolls and throws and breakfalls
Do not depend on any sort of weapon,
But only on what I might coin a phrase and call
The ever-important question of human balance,
And the ever-important need to be in a strong
　　Position at the start.

There are many kinds of weakness about the body,
Where you would least expect, like the ball of the foot.
But the various holds and rolls and throws and breakfalls
Will always come in useful. And never be frightened
To tackle from behind: it may not be clean to do so,
　　But this is global war.

So give them all you have, and always give them
As good as you get; it will always get you somewhere.
(You may not know it, but you can tie a Jerry
Up without rope; it is one of the things I shall teach you.)
Nothing will matter if only you are ready for him.
　　The readiness is all.

The readiness is all. How can I help but feel
I have been here before? But somehow then,
I was the tied-up one. How to get out
Was always then my problem. And even if I had
A piece of rope I was always the sort of person
    Who threw the rope aside.

And in my time I have given them all I had,
Which was never as good as I got, and it got me nowhere.
And the various holds and rolls and throws and breakfalls
Somehow or other I always seemed to put
In the wrong place. And as for war, my wars
    Were global from the start.

Perhaps I was never in a strong position,
Or the ball of my foot got hurt, or I had some weakness
Where I had least expected. But I think I see your point.
While awaiting a proper issue, we must learn the lesson
Of the ever-important question of human balance.
    It is courage that counts.

Things may be the same again; and we must fight
Not in the hope of winning but rather of keeping
Something alive: so that when we meet our end,
It may be said that we tackled wherever we could,
That battle-fit we lived, and though defeated,
    Not without glory fought.

Naming of Parts must be one of the most widely known poems of
the Second World War, but its companion pieces ought to
accompany it for the sake of completeness; and the whole se-
quence is particularly welcome in an anthology which would
otherwise be rather deficient in wit and humour.

Lessons of the War illustrates perfectly the attitude of the poet in
uniform who tries to establish his "point of balance" in an un-
sympathetic and insensitive military world. In these poems that

world is represented by the hard, mechanically uttered, semi-literate expressions of the sergeant-major who is instructing his men in the technicalities of modern war. The tone and phrasing of these are beautifully caught (as will be recognized by anyone who was conscripted into the armed forces during or after the Second World War), and they are incorporated with skilful facility into the poem. In contrast, there are the musings of the private soldier reacting to the words of instruction, deliberately setting the world as he sees it in human and personal terms against the impersonal world of military jargon. The connection between the two worlds is made by the use of ambiguities: "Which in your case you have not got"; "easing the spring"; "There may be dead ground in between"; "the ever-important need to be in a strong position" and "while awaiting a proper issue" are all examples of expressions which are given an ironic twist so that they can be turned away from the sergeant-major's world and related to the personal and private thoughts of the poet. Much of the sardonic humour and wit of the poems arises from these ironic ambiguities, but some of the irony is of a self-mocking kind, and some of the humour is at the writer's own expense. The self-examination involved in this attitude is brought out most clearly in the last poem, *Unarmed Combat*, where a tone of seriousness is introduced with the recognition of the quotation from *Hamlet*: "The readiness is all" is spoken by the acutely introspective Prince at a moment when he has come to accept the inevitability of death and is prophetically aware of its closeness. The mood of this poem does not attempt to match the solemnity of Hamlet's situation, for the tone of self-disparagement continues, but at the end of the poem seriousness returns with

> we must learn the lesson
> Of the ever-important question of human balance . . .

and

> we must fight
> Not in the hope of winning but rather of keeping
> Something alive . . .

so that when the final words of the sequence are reached we find

that we can interpret the poem's epigraph* in a slightly less
ironical way than at first seemed appropriate.

RANDALL JARRELL (1914–1965)

EIGHTH AIR FORCE

IF, in an odd angle of the hutment,
A puppy laps the water from a can
Of flowers, and the drunk sergeant shaving
Whistles *O Paradiso!*—shall I say that man
Is not as men have said: a wolf to man?

The other murderers troop in yawning;
Three of them play Pitch, one sleeps, and one
Lies counting missions, lies there sweating
Till even his heart beats: One; One; One.
O murderers! . . . Still, this is how it's done:

This is a war. . . . But since these play, before they die,
Like puppies with their puppy; since, a man,
I did as these have done, but did not die—
I will content the people as I can
And give up these to them: Behold the man!

I have suffered, in a dream, because of him,
Many things; for this last saviour, man,
I have lied as I lie now. But what is lying?
Men wash their hands, in blood, as best they can:
I find no fault in this just man.

---

* The lines are from Horace, and the quotation usually reads, "*Vixi
puellis* . . .". Here it means, "I have lived until recently a competent soldier,
and have served not without glory".

In this poem, Jarrell, who served in the United States Army
Air Force from 1942–6, is concerned with the question of the
guilt or innocence of combatants in war. Innocence is represented
by the puppy and the men who play with it; but the men are
"murderers", for they are aircrew back from a bombing mission,
and appear to be indifferent to their situation, except for the one
who is afraid. The poet now associates himself with the men, for
he is one of them, and asks if, in the circumstances of war, they
can be condemned as guilty. From this point onwards the poem
relates the question of the men's guilt or innocence to the Gospels'
accounts of Christ's appearance before Pilate (see Matthew, 27;
Mark, 15; Luke, 23; John, 18). The men must be found guilty,
for, in order to "content the people", a scapegoat must be found.
But, like Pilate, the poet is uneasy about this condemnation, for
he has convinced himself of the innocence of "the man"; and,
like Pilate's wife, he has "suffered, in a dream, because of him",
and he has lied for him. (Pilate's question, "What is truth?"
becomes "What is lying?") In the final lines he declares the
innocence of "the man", but the ritual washing of the hands as a
symbol of exoneration is performed not in water but in blood, so
that at the end of the poem a deliberately ambiguous effect is
created, and, in spite of the authoritative last line, we are left to
conclude that the men—all men—are essentially guilty.

In spite of the sombre tone, which is emphasized by the
narrowly restricted rhyme-scheme, this is a powerfully dramatic
poem, with its juxtaposition of the scene at the Air Force base
and that at the trial of Christ, for out of the fusing of these two
images arises Jarrell's conception of the combatant as both
murderer and victim (compare Sassoon's simpler allusion to the
Christ-figure in *The Redeemer* (p. 83)); and the fact that this
dilemma is not resolved leaves us with a sense of the poet's com-
passion for man with his burden of moral responsibility.

LOUIS MACNEICE (1907–1963)

CONVOY

TOGETHER, keeping in line, slow as if hypnotised
Across the blackboard sea in sombre echelon
The food-ships draw their wakes. No Euclid could have devised
Neater means to a more essential end—
Unless the chalk breaks off, the convoy is surprised.

The cranks go up and down, the smoke trails tendril out,
The precious cargoes creak, the signals clack,
All is under control and nobody need shout,
We are steady as we go, and on our flanks
The little whippet warships romp and scurry about.

This is a bit like us: the individual sets
A course for all his soul's more basic needs
Of love and pride-of-life, but sometimes he forgets
How much their voyage home depends upon pragmatic
And ruthless attitudes—destroyers and corvettes.

MacNeice's poem provides another example of the deliberately
detached manner, the purposeful coolness, of much of the poetry
of the Second World War. In the first stanza the convoy is seen
at a distance: photographed, as it were, from an aerial view-point,
and the coolness is emphasized grammatically by the withhold-
ing of the main verb in the first sentence and emotionally by the
use of a geometrical image, suggesting the formal demonstration
of a theorem in the lecture room. In the second stanza the camera
moves in for a close-up shot of the ships where "All is under
control", "We are steady as we go", and the merchant navy
tradition of orderly efficiency is indicated with appropriate

economy. But at the end of each of these stanzas there is a hint of a possible disturbance of this orderliness: "Unless the chalk breaks off", and the presence of the warships—deceptively gay in appearance—imply the hidden threat of a U-boat attack, and it is this idea of sudden emergency that MacNeice develops as a kind of moral in the last stanza. The "moral" is introduced almost apologetically, with a rather self-conscious colloquialism, but the point is made, neatly and without fuss, that life often demands "pragmatic and ruthless attitudes", and is made the more effectively because of the sense of restraint that has controlled the poem throughout.

CHARLES CAUSLEY (BORN 1917)

DEATH OF AN AIRCRAFT
An Incident of the Cretan Campaign, 1941
(To George Psychoundakis)

ONE day on our village in the month of July
An aeroplane sank from the sea of the sky,
    White as a whale it smashed on the shore
    Bleeding oil and petrol all over the floor.

The Germans advanced in the vertical heat
To save the dead plane from the people of Crete,
    And round the glass wreck in a circus of snow
    Set seven mechanical sentries to go.

Seven stalking spiders about the sharp sun
Clicking like clockwork and each with a gun,
    But at *Come to the Cookhouse* they wheeled about
    And sat down to sausages and sauerkraut.

Down from the mountain burning so brown
Wriggled three heroes from Kastelo town,
    Deep in the sand they silently sank
    And each struck a match for a petrol-tank.

Up went the plane in a feather of fire
As the bubbling boys began to retire
    And, grey in the guardhouse, seven Berliners
    Lost their stripes as well as their dinners.

Down in the village, at murder-stations,
The Germans fell in friends and relations:
    But not a Kastelian snapped an eye
    As he spat in the air and prepared to die.

Not a Kastelian whispered a word
Dressed with the dust to be massacred,
    And squinted up at the sky with a frown
    As three bubbly boys came walking down.

One was sent to the county gaol
Too young for bullets if not for bail,
    But the other two were in prime condition
    To take on a load of ammunition.

In Archontiki they stood in the weather
Naked, hungry, chained together:
    Stark as the stones in the market-place,
    Under the eyes of the populace.

Their irons unlocked as their naked hearts
They faced the squad and their funeral-carts.
    The Captain cried, "Before you're away
    Is there any last word you'd like to say?"

"I want no words," said one, "with my lead,
Only some water to cool my head."
    "Water," the other said, "is all very fine
    But I'll be taking a glass of wine.

"A glass of wine for the afternoon
With permission to sing a signature-tune!"
    And he ran the *raki* down his throat
    And took a deep breath for the leading note.

But before the squad could shoot or say
Like the impala he leapt away
    Over the rifles, under the biers,
    The bullets rattling round his ears.

"Run!" they cried to the boy of stone
Who now stood there in the street alone,
    But, "Rather than bring revenge on your head
    It is better for me to die," he said.

The soldiers turned their machine-guns round
And shot him down with a dreadful sound
    Scrubbed his face with perpetual dark
    And rubbed it out like a pencil mark.

But his comrade slept in the olive tree
And sailed by night on the gnawing sea,
    The soldier's silver shilling earned
    And, armed like an archangel, returned.

Death of an Aircraft is the only unmistakably violent poem included amongst those representing the Second World War, but its consciously unromantic, brutal treatment of an heroic story could be seen as another method of dealing in an objective manner with the enormities of war, for by imposing upon the language and rhythm of the verse something of the ruthlessness of the episode, Causley retains a firm control over the subject-matter. He describes the incident with an air of savage indifference, as if determined not to be moved by feats of courage and self-sacrifice, and to this is added a rough and grotesque kind of humour (mainly at the expense of the German occupying forces), which also helps to suppress any latent heroics. The total effect, therefore, is one of tough nonchalance; but despite the hardness and assumed attitude of indifference, or perhaps because of it, the climax of the poem, when the boy refuses to save himself—

> Rather than bring revenge on your head
> It is better for me to die . . .

stands out as unashamedly heroic, and the remaining two stanzas, describing the pitiless killing of the boy—"Scrubbed his face with perpetual dark"—and his comrade's return, "armed like an archangel", possess a quality of almost epic excitement which appears to contradict the tone of what has preceded them. When one recalls that the poem is called not *Death of a Hero* but *Death of an Aircraft* the excitement may become more subdued, but the technique that Causley employs (owing something perhaps to Kipling and to the ballad-poems of W. H. Auden) enables him to produce a momentary heroic effect out of verse whose predominant quality is an apparently cynical, thrusting directness. The poem has nothing of the coolness noted in *Lessons of the War* (p. 117) or in *Convoy*, but through its vigorous realism it preserves its own kind of detachment.

(It may be interesting to compare the treatment of heroism in this poem with that accorded to a simpler kind in the Border ballads (pp. 13–27) and to a more sophisticated variety in *The Nabara* (p. 99).)

BARRY AMIEL (BORN 1921)

DEATH IS A MATTER OF MATHEMATICS

Death is a matter of mathematics.

It screeches down at you from dirtywhite nothingness
And your life is a question of velocity and altitude,
With allowances for wind and the quick, relentless pull
Of gravity.

6 Or else it lies concealed
7 In that fleecy, peaceful puff of cloud ahead,
8 A streamlined, muttering vulture, waiting
9 To swoop upon you with a rush of steel.
10 And then your chances vary as the curves
11 Of your parabolas, your banks, your dives,
12 The scientific soundness of your choice
13 Of what to push or pull, and how, and when.
14 Or perhaps you walk oblivious in a wood,
15 Or crawl flat-bellied over pockmarked earth,
16 And Death awaits you in a field-gray tunic.
17 Sights upright and aligned. Range estimated
18 And set in. A lightning, subconscious calculation
19 Of trajectory and deflection. With you the focal point,
20 The centre of the problem. The A and B
21 Or Smith and Jones of schoolboy textbooks.

22 Ten out of ten means you are dead.

Barry Amiel is not a professional writer. He wrote this poem when, as a young anti-aircraft officer in the Second World War, he had attended a lecture on the mathematics of gunnery and was given "ten out of ten" for producing the correct solution to a trigonometrical problem. The poem evolved from this simple incident.

Like Reed's *Lessons of the War* (p. 117), it is concerned with the business of training for war rather than with fighting, so its air of detachment is not surprising, but it illustrates very vividly the attitude of quiet, unemotional reflection that arises from a recognition of the scientific nature of modern warfare. Death from the air, death in the air and death from the ground: each is considered in turn, and each is the result of a careful calculation and the accurate manipulation of precision instruments. There are no real people in the poem: death comes from "A streamlined muttering vulture", and the nearest thing to a human being is "a field-gray tunic". When the calculation is correct, a man dies. (Compare the following lines from *The Nabara* (p. 102):

Aboard *Canarias* the German gun-layers stationed
Brisk at their intricate batteries—guns and men both trained
To a hair in accuracy, aimed at a pitiless end. . . .)

This conception of modern war as "a matter of mathematics"
gives a new meaning to the word "inhumanity", for the ability to
destroy an enemy from many miles away, although not a new
technique, makes the killing impersonal, something remote from
immediate contact, so that any sense of responsibility for inflicting
death and wounds becomes weakened and therefore easier to
tolerate. Since this poem was written, death has become still more
scientifically a matter of mathematics, but some years before the
arrival of intercontinental ballistic missiles Amiel described,
simply and effectively, man's most recently developed capacity
for killing his fellow men. The terse conclusion, ironically evoking
the school classroom, renders moral comment unnecessary, but
perhaps such comment is implicit in the poem.

RUTHVEN TODD (BORN 1914)

THESE ARE FACTS

THESE are facts, observe them how you will:
Forget for a moment the medals and the glory,
The clean shape of the bomb, designed to kill,
And the proud headlines of the papers' story.

Remember the walls of brick that forty years
Had nursed to make a neat though shabby home;
The impertinence of death, ignoring tears,
That smashed the house and left untouched the Dome.

Bodies in death are not magnificent or stately,
Bones are not elegant that blast has shattered;
This sorry, stained and crumpled rag was lately
A man whose life was made of little things that mattered;

Now he is just a nuisance, liable to stink,
A breeding-ground for flies, a test-tube for disease:
Bury him quickly and never pause to think,
What is the future worth to men like these?

People are more than places, more than pride;
A million photographs record the works of Wren;
A city remains a city on credit from the tide
That flows among its rocks, a sea of men.

Ruthven Todd's poem is the only one in this section concerned with the suffering of civilians in war, and the only one which might be described as a poem of protest. Its subject is the brutal incursion of war into people's everyday experience. After putting aside the public and official aspects—the medals, the headlines—the writer turns to the personal, first with the reference to the smashed house, and then with the shattered bodies which were once as alive as we are and have now been reduced to the "stained and crumpled rag", to be buried as quickly as possible: "These are facts." Todd's protest is directed against those who would value "the works of Wren" more highly than the lives and homes of ordinary human beings, for during the bombing of London in the Second World War, the dome of St. Paul's cathedral, standing almost unscathed amid the surrounding destruction, became a symbol of the city's capacity for survival under concentrated aerial attack, and Todd believed that "People are more than places". The indignation he experienced is powerfully communicated, but for all its harsh realism it is expressed with restraint, and the poem's quietly dignified manner (the pace checked by the occasional inclusion of an extra foot in the line) makes an effective plea for a sense of perspective in wartime, for fear we should exalt national pride above the suffering of war's victims.

Peter Porter (born 1929)

YOUR ATTENTION PLEASE

Your attention please—
The Polar DEW* has just warned that
A nuclear rocket strike of
At least one thousand megatons
Has been launched by the enemy
Directly at our major cities.
This announcement will take
Two and a quarter minutes to make,
You therefore have a further
Eight and a quarter minutes
To comply with the shelter
Requirements published in the Civil
Defence Code—section Atomic Attack.
A specially shortened Mass
Will be broadcast at the end
Of this announcement—
Protestant and Jewish services
Will begin simultaneously—
Select your wavelength immediately
According to instructions
In the Defence Code. Do not
Take well-loved pets (including birds)
Into your shelter—they will consume
Fresh air. Leave the old and bed-
ridden, you can do nothing for them.

---

* "Distant Early Warning": a system of radar stations designed to pick up
signals from an approaching enemy missile attack.

Remember to press the sealing
Switch when everyone is in
The shelter. Set the radiation
Aerial, turn on the geiger barometer.
Turn off your Television now.
Turn off your radio immediately
The Services end. At the same time
Secure explosion plugs in the ears
Of each member of your family. Take
Down your plasma flasks. Give your children
The pills marked one and two
In the C.D. green container, then put
Them to bed. Do not break
The inside airlock seals until
The radiation All Clear shows
(Watch for the cuckoo in your
perspex panel), or your District
Touring Doctor rings your bell.
If before this your air becomes
Exhausted or if any of your family
Is critically injured, administer
The capsules marked "Valley Forge"*
(Red pocket in No. I Survival Kit)
For painless death. (Catholics
Will have been instructed by their priests
What to do in this eventuality.)
This announcement is ending. Our President
Has already given orders for
Massive retaliation—it will be
Decisive. Some of us may die.
Remember, statistically

---

* The name, used in this context, will have ironic associations for those familiar with American history, for it was in Valley Forge, Pennsylvania, that General Washington's army of 10,000 men camped in the winter of 1777–8 (after the British had occupied Philadelphia) and suffered privations of hunger and cold through official mismanagement of supplies.

It is not likely to be you.
All flags are flying fully dressed
On Government buildings—the sun is shining.
Death is the least we have to fear.
We are all in the hands of God,
Whatever happens happens by His Will.
Now go quickly to your shelters.

PETER APPLETON (BORN 1925)

THE RESPONSIBILITY

I AM the man who gives the word,
If it should come, to use the Bomb.

I am the man who spreads the word
From him to them if it should come.

I am the man who gets the word
From him who spreads the word from him.

I am the man who drops the Bomb
If ordered by the one who's heard
From him who merely spreads the word
The first one gives if it should come.

I am the man who loads the Bomb
That he must drop should orders come
From him who gets the word passed on
By one who waits to hear from *him*.

I am the man who makes the Bomb
That he must load for him to drop
If told by one who gets the word
From one who passes it from *him*.

I am the man who fills the till,
Who pays the tax, who foots the bill
That guarantees the Bomb he makes
For him to load for him to drop
If orders come from one who gets
The word passed on to him by one
Who waits to hear it from the man
Who gives the word to use the Bomb.

I am the man behind it all;
I am the one responsible.

The last two poems in this selection concern the war which
hasn't happened, the nuclear war which to most people is un-
thinkable because either they cannot imagine it could take place
or the thought of it is intolerable. Both Porter and Appleton try
to face the question of such a war and express an attitude towards
it which is ruthlessly honest. In order to do this, each adopts a
particular tone of voice.

The voice in Porter's poem could perhaps be taken for that of a
familiar radio-announcer whose tone is not only one of authority
but of reassurance at a time of crisis. In spite of the cataclysmic
nature of the announcement, the voice remains calm, and issues
its instructions with careful precision. Every eventuality has been
catered for; no detail has been overlooked. Provided the instruc-
tions are properly followed, there will be no need for anxiety, and
we can retire to our shelters, after due religious observance, in the
assurance that everything will be all right.

But the more we hear of this voice, the more it becomes that of
a machine, a harsh mechanical sound which is no longer recog-
nizably human. The relentlessly issued series of instructions have
a certain hollowness about them, and we begin to react with
horror rather than with a sense of reassurance. We realize that
the carefully considered directions contain advice on the abandon-
ment of the old and sick and the killing of our children, and that
the provision of religious services, as an officially approved opiate,

is a mockery. The comfort we take in the news that massive retaliation has been ordered, that the flags are flying and the sun shining, becomes a bitter realization that such things no longer matter, and that if "death is the least we have to fear" then the worst must be of immeasurable horror.

The inexorable movement of the verse, with its coldly efficient utterance and official jargon, suggests the inhuman attitudes which could create the circumstances for such an announcement to be appropriate, and could envisage nuclear war as a tolerable experience for mankind. This is a cruel and brutal poem, but one which has a terrifying relevance for the contemporary world.

The voice in Appleton's poem has an even more disarming tone than that which at first seemed to be heard in *Your Attention Please*, for it is that of the nursery rhyme. The pattern of "This is the House that Jack Built", with its succession of adjectival clauses, is adopted here to suggest a naïvety of manner which, as the sentences develop in complexity and the pronouns become more difficult to identify, becomes comic, so that we forget for a moment the horrifying simplicity of the opening couplet. The complications continue up to the eight-line stanza, where the sequence of relatives and antecedents is so involved that the reader's sense of humour is held in check only by the ominous recurrence of the word "Bomb". But there is no room to doubt Appleton's seriousness in the final couplet, for out of the confusion of accountability comes the stark directness of "I am the one responsible".

The poem makes two points very effectively. First is the statement that we are all responsible for the manufacture and possible use of the Bomb, however removed we may seem to be from the immediate onus of direct responsibility. Second, the very confusion exemplified in the poem's structure suggests the ease with which we can all shrug off this responsibility and pass it on to the next man who seems to be more personally involved than we are. The immensely complicated nature of modern society and the scientific nature of modern warfare increase the individual's feeling of being out of touch with any immediate responsibility for what happens, and this poem, while illustrating the complexity of the situation, brings home to us the uncomfortable reality of the burden we all have to bear.

INDEX OF AUTHORS

INDEX OF FIRST LINES